Ways to Play:
recreation alternatives

edited by James C. McCullagh

with contributions from:

Paul Hogan
Malcolm Wells
Bernie DeKoven
Esther Frankel
Waldo Nielsen
Caroline Ringo
Ann Buxbaum

Rodale Press, Emmaus, Pa.

Library of Congress Cataloging in Publication Data
Main entry under title:

Ways to play.

   1. Recreation—United States—Addresses, essays,
lectures. 2. Recreation—Addresses, essays, lectures.
3. Play—History—Addresses, essays, lectures.
4. Recreation areas—United States—Addresses, essays,
lectures. 5. Recreation areas—Addresses, essays,
lectures. I. McCullagh, James C. II. Hogan, Paul.
GV53.W38   790'.0973   77-29228
ISBN 0-87857-226-0

*Printed in the United States of America on recycled paper
containing a high percentage of de-inked fiber.*

2   4   6   8   10   9   7   5   3   1

Contents

Paul Hogan

Play in History
Play in Colonial America
Play Today
Play at Home
Community Play
The Evolution of a Playground
Planning for Play

James C. McCullagh

Allegory from the Grave
Evanston, Illinois
Miamisburg, Ohio
Seattle, Washington
Los Angeles County, California

James C. McCullagh

Recreation and the Community
The Staten Island Greenbelt Trail
Discovering Trails Close to Home

III

IV   WAYS TO PLAY

C. Lloyd W. Jones
D. Larry Pichman
E. Harriett E. Milbourn

Caroline Ringo

A Sport for All Ages
Equipment
The First Meet
The Chase
Starting from Scratch

Esther Frankel

The Complete Dance
The First Step
A Communal Activity

Bernie DeKoven

Cultures and Competitions
Right in Your Own Backyard or Your Attic, or Your
Basement, or the Street:
    The Idea; The Principle; The Guarantee;
    Preparation; Equipment; Food; Drink; The
    Invitation; The Place; The People; The Time;
    Starting; The Arts; Donations; Ending It;
    Resources; Love.
New Games from Old
    Size of Areas; Number; Object Thrown; Number
    of Objects; Nature of Boundaries; Success;
    Result of Success
Free-Form Frisbee Golf
    Official Rules: The Game for One; Official Rules
    of Free-Form Frisbee Golf for a Few; Some
    Intriguing Ramifications
Playing Together
    Ping-Pong; Socks; Baseball
The Games Preserve
A Town of Players

VI   WAYS TO PLAY

Acknowledgments

I would like to thank the individual contributors, each of whom has left his special mark on this book. I am grateful to the readers of *Prevention, Organic Gardening and Farming, National Parks and Conservation Magazine,* and a number of running magazines, who shared their thoughts about "play" with us; to Tom Yoannou and Tom Floyd who provided information about building trails; to Mark Wall for his help in preparing "The Cycle"; to Bob McCray for his report on Mt. Trashmore; to Dr. Friedrich Schneider for his ideas about "discovering" exercise courses close to home; to Bob and Janet Putnam, Bob Walk, and Hugh MacMullan and children for contributions to "The Chase"; to the various bicycle riders for their accounts of touring; to James J. Berryhill for his suggestions about self-help bikeways; and to John Henry Norton for his help in preparing "The Ball."

My thanks to Tom Gettings, Margaret Smyser, and John Hamil of the Rodale Photo Lab who took most of the photographs for the book. And to Alice Nass for her good research and assistance.

James C. McCullagh

Introduction

This book is about play and recreation. Not the kind that one experiences from the yard markers or feet away from the deep glow of the television screen. But about organic play, which might be loosely described as a kind of recreational activity that proceeds from within an individual, a family, a community.

The basic theme of the book, presented playfully and anecdotally, is that we have as much responsibility to look after the recreation needs of ourselves and our children as we do to look after our personal health and well-being.

Today, recreation is becoming a more significant (and less significant) part of our lives. We have more leisure time—or so we are told. Thus in most metropolitan areas, the weekend opens with a roar, as half-empty cars rush painstakingly toward leisure. Seymour Gold, professor of environmental planning at the University of California, Davis, writes that "the amount of time people spend traveling to a day-use region area generally equals the amount of time they spend on-site. Hence, a two-hour picnic normally implies an hour of travel each way and an estimated round trip of 50 to 100 miles in most urban areas. Reduced speed limits to conserve energy, increasing levels of traffic congestion, and the termination of massive freeway construction programs will discourage convenient automobile access to regional and remote parks."

Gold speculates that "decreasing levels of disposable and real income, and increasing levels of unemployment and inflation, will lessen the demand for high-cost activities such as power boating, visits to resorts, skiing, and European vacations. Conversely, the demand should be increased for simple, low-cost activities close to home such as walking, bicycling, swimming, and canoeing.

"The increased cost of gasoline or the prospect of fuel rationing may force many people to drastically change their priorities and seek energy-conserving ways to spend their leisure time in or near cities. The option of personal transportation will be replaced with mass transit alternatives or bicycle or pedestrian access to local recreation opportunities."

Whether the scenario painted by Gold ever comes to pass remains to be seen. Nonetheless, it does raise some interesting questions and possibilities. The implication is that recreation should no longer be considered a personal thing, a quest to travel the farthest distance in a weekend, to conquer another frontier; the one who seeks recreation cannot move without affecting others. Our recreation habits collectively bear on the quality of life of the nation.

Henry Fairlie notes in the *Washington Post* that "Americans in their hundreds of thousands now sail in the great bays and estuaries of their country; they get there by car. They now backpack in the wilderness and in the mountains; they get there by car. They now kayak on their rivers; they get there by car. They now ski down the slopes of their country and climb them in summer; they get there by car. They go to their beaches to swim or to laze; they get there by car. They go to the desert in spring and find its beauties; they get there by car. Even in the cities during the week, they go increasingly to tennis courts, swimming pools and golf courses; they get there often by car.

"They need gasoline to get to the places where they can do what needs no gasoline. There is nothing more galling than meeting a backpacker in the mountains, enjoying his high with nature, complaining about the dreadfulness of civilization that allows so many cars to make so many fumes and to use so much energy—and then watch him at the foot of the mountain calmly get into the Datsun which has brought him there, to drive back home in the serene and uncomplicated belief that at least his fumes have been for a worthy purpose."

Fairlie's tongue-in-cheek description of a heady backpacker does have a ring of truth to it. And this is true of so many recreation pursuits. For example, the Interior Department estimates that more than 90 percent of all national park visitors arrive in automobiles. Moreover, "approximately 75 percent of all national park visitors are members of the 15 percent upper-income segment of the population."

The primary objective of this book is not necessarily to discourage people from using cars to get to far-away vacation lands —although that would be a happy outcome. The main objective is to suggest ways, through personal experiences, anecdotes, and germane examples of individuals and communities, for people to depend on their own resources for their recreation and play.

Moreover, individual authors remind us that we have a responsibility to the recreation spaces in our community; that helping to plan or build or maintain a recreation space can itself be a type of recreation. In the chapter entitled "The Play," Paul Hogan takes us into the world of children's play and shows ways in which we can participate in community-generated parks and playgrounds. Numerous individuals and groups across the country have participated in the recreation process this way. And, as Hogan notes, understanding the play needs of children will help us better understand our own needs. This is organic play: activities and spaces articulated from within.

Clearly, one of the book's aims is to extend conventional definitions of recreation to include the actual building of community spaces. The account of Frances Young in chapter two, who turned a trash heap into a beautiful botanical garden, should lend credibility to such a definition. Undeniably, Mrs. Young got her pleasure and recreation from spearheading the project. And her pleasure is the community's space. In fact, the entire chapter outlining examples of "recycling the community for play" has an organic ring to it: Out of nothing, comes play. Out of an individual's and a community's efforts comes recreation space.

Similarly, the chapters dealing with the "building of trails in your own backyard" invite the reader to become involved in these activities. And here, unmistakably, conservation and personal responsibility are wedded to the idea of recreation. Justice William O. Douglas, in his prepared speech at the dedication of the Chesapeake & Ohio Canal, acknowledges the importance of saving the little green we have in our backyard:

"Harry Golden, the owner and publisher of the *Israelite* in North Carolina, was raised in the lower east side of Manhattan. In one of his writings he wrote a line that was very moving to me.

He said that in front of his New York house there was a crack in the sidewalk and in that crack, 23 blades of grass had grown and they were bright and refreshing.

"We Americans often think in terms of thousands of acres when we think of the wilderness but Harry Golden's wilderness was 23 blades of grass, and can be made available to almost any city dweller. Smaller things are sometimes the most beautiful of all."

Interestingly, Justice Douglas invokes the "smallness" concept in the recreation field, suggesting perhaps that we consider our "backyards" as spaces for play.

Seymour Gold, referred to earlier, takes the argument a little further—and notes these changes in the recreation movement in this country, particularly as applied to urban areas.

1. Recycling urban parks in the same way we recycle newspaper or glass is the only strategy for many communities, and makes sense.
2. The philosophy of alternative, noncompetitive recreation programs such as New Games is the wave of the future. A rapidly changing philosophy of competition is already challenging the Little League's popularity in many communities.
3. A new spirit of self-help, community involvement, and consciousness is emerging in many places. The spirit recognizes the limits of government in solving many human problems.

Even a casual observer who notices the joggers, the cyclists, the New Games activities, might sense this new spirit. And those who are fortunate enough to know of specific communities imbued with a "new spirit of self-help" know with certainty that a new consciousness is emerging.

In light of these developments (and these hopes) this book explores the recreation aspects of both the play and the space. The early chapters provide concrete examples of individuals and communities who have "taken charge of their recreation fate" by getting involved in parks, gardens, and playspaces. The aim of these examples is clearly to motivate the reader to do likewise. Again, creating playspaces can indeed be a kind of recreation.

The second half of the book explores, largely through personal experiences and anecdotes, a number of play activities which tend to be lifelong, family-oriented, and active: bicycling, orienteering, running, family games, folk dancing, hocker (a cross between soccer and field hockey), as well as ingenious play activities invented by people across the country. And the last chapter, written by Malcolm Wells, extends the concept of organic play a little further.

We hope that *Ways to Play* motivates readers to take an active part in their recreation, whether it means "building" a bike trail in the community or discovering forms of recreation for themselves and their families.

Equally important, we hope you find the book enjoyable; it is filled with accounts of people who have new and interesting views about play and recreation. Like them, we hope you will play your way into paradise.

chapter 1

The Play

by Paul Hogan

The word play has about twoscore definitions in Webster's dictionary. Everyone talks about play, but little is done to promote it. The United Nations Declaration of the Rights of the Child states, "The child shall have full opportunity for play and recreation, which should be directed to the same purpose as education: society and the public authorities shall endeavour to promote the employment of this right."

Ian Fletcher, who edits *It's Child's Play,* a London-based bimonthly magazine, offers this definition of play: "Play involves children in freely chosen activities which develop skills, enables them to learn about relationships with their fellows and increases understanding of their character and potential. Play is ideal education for life with scope for enterprise, imagination, social contracts and the need for rules."

To go back a few thousand years, Aristophanes tells of children who made their own toys. He mentions ships and even frogs made of pomegranate peels. The Greek children played outdoor games of odd or even, slap in the dark, hunt the slipper, catch ball, hide and seek, heads or tails and almost all the games children have played in the intervening twenty-five centuries.

In his early years, Plato insisted that the rules of children's games be made inviolate and change forbidden. In his middle years he still felt such restrictions against change would make the citizen less prone to violate the laws of the city-state.

As Plato grew older and yet more wise, he pronounced about toys in the nursery. He spoke against having too many toys as discouraging originality. He advocated mimic tools for carpen-

1

tering and encouraged free play, "those natural modes of amusement which children find out for themselves when they meet."

To go back a few more millennia, the Bible tells us in Zachariah 8:5, "And the streets of the city shall be full of boys and girls playing in the streets thereof."

We could go back to Egyptian times and their drawings of children playing the same games we do today. Doubtless, we will uncover yet older references to children's play as we dig deeper into our past.

But what of the present and the future of play? Today, playing in the streets can be hazardous to your health. Once-empty streets are choked with parked and moving cars. Once-empty lots are jammed with either high-rise apartments or trash and sometimes it's hard to tell the difference. Once-beauti-

1-1: Model airplane built from logs appears in Paris playground.
(Courtesy of Jeanmarie Bresson)

1-2: Children from Christ-church, New Zealand, play house in a packing-crate village.
(Courtesy of J. C. Parker)

1-3: Peter Ward and his son Murray erecting a new stairway to the children's play hut at the J. R. McKenzie kindergarten in Christ-church, New Zealand.
(Courtesy of J. C. Parker)

ful parks are lairs for monsters. The one very basic missing ingredient is humanity. People are missing. People are missing from the entire concept of playgrounds, from the first idea to the planning and construction, and certainly through the operation and maintenance of any recreational facility. *What is needed is a return to the old-fashioned open space where the community decides what they want to do, how they want to do it, and proceeds to recreate their environment according to their recreational needs.*

So, like it or not, children are still playing Aprdidrskinds (hide and seek) and Chytinda (frog in the middle) and Dielkustinda (tug of war). The architects, equipment manufacturers and recreation leaders who foist the concrete turtle playground on us must eventually fail. But what a difficult time this is right now. How can those of us who want to give play back to the children and not make a multibillion-dollar industry hope to succeed against such formidable odds? A long process of re-education is needed. A commitment must be made.

My own two earliest recollections were going to work with my father and beachcombing with my mother. My father was a house builder and I played in his sand pile, collected dropped nails and pieces of 2 x 4s and created boats, houses, towns and new worlds. My mother and I walked the beach at dawn and found seashells, toys left behind from the day before or washed up with the tide. In my child's mind it seemed we did this every single morning for years. Such is the impression of youth. Most likely we beachcombed just a few times. But what an impression it made.

My life is still devoted to building and beachcombing in all its myriad forms. To build and create from found objects, from the surplus of our society, from nothing, is a constant dream fulfillment for me. Out of nothing can come play.

Play in History

As we wander through the centuries in the history of play one thing is constant, the way in which children play. John Froissart wrote of his happy childhood in the fourteenth century. In one of his poems he listed fifty-two childhood games he played.

He chased butterflies, threw feathers into the wind, blew bubbles and played prisoner's base.

That boys played truant in the fifteenth century is made clear by the following poem:

> I would my master were a hare
> And all his bookes houndes were
> And I myself a jolly hunter
> To blow my horn I would not spare!
> For if he were dead I would not care.

Most of the games of the Middle Ages were real-life sports such as riding, hunting, hawking, tilting at the quintain on a wooden horse, etc. As through most of history, children's play was a preparation for the rigors of adulthood. Schoolchildren of the Middle Ages used hornbooks. These books were usually a sheet of paper on which was written the alphabet, a short story or a moral admonition. The paper was pasted on a flat board and covered with a thin slice of horn to protect it from both the children and the elements.

One such hornbook which survived the children and the centuries tells us of games played in 1611:

> To wrestle, play at stooletballe, or to
> pitch the barre, or to shoote off a gunne
> To play at loggats, nine hold, or ten pinnes
> To try it out at footballe by the shinnes.

Hopscotch was known as "Scotch hoppers" in early Pennsylvania. The game "I catch you without green" was mentioned by Rabelais. It is still played in the Carolinas. I played it as "red rover" in Philadelphia forty years ago. Stone tag and wood tap was played in Elizabethan days. The player is tagged "it" if he or she falls off a stone. Cat's cradle must have been invented the day after string arrived.

Play in Colonial America

A pre-Revolutionary War book, *The Pretty Little Pocket-Book* is in the rare book section of the Philadelphia Free Library.

It is under lock and key and I had the privilege of looking at it. They would not allow me to take photographs, but the book has detailed drawings showing how games were played. Such pastimes as chuck-farthing, kite flying, may-pole, marbles, hops and hide, thread the needle, fishing, blindman's bluff, shuttle cock, kind as I, peg-farthing, knock out a span, hop, skip and jump, boys and girls come out to play, I sent a letter to my love, cricket, stool-ball, base-ball, trap ball, swimming, tip-cat, train branding, pitch and hassel, fives, leap frog, bird watching, hop hut, shooting, hopscotch, squares, and riding rosemary tree are mentioned. The beautiful thing about this book is that the directions on how to play the various games are all in rhyme.

CHUCK-FARTHING
As you value your pence
At the hole take your aim
Chuck all safely in
And you'd win the game.

'MORAL'
Chuck-Farthing, like trade
requires great care.
The more you observe,
The better you fare.

The games and the poetic directions on how to play them all had a moral. The early founders and their children left little to chance. There was a purpose to every facet of their life—even children's play.

Children's Games by Pieter Brueghel the Elder more graphically depicts the way children played in the sixteenth century than all the books I have read on that period. The painting, originally titled *Summer,* belonged to a cycle which included *The Fight Between Carnival and Lent, Ice-Skating* and *Fair at Hoboken.* All four paintings pictured amusements which were popular, and each represented one of the seasons.

There are more than a hundred different games illustrated in Brueghel's masterpiece. Hoops, pin-the-tail-on-the-donkey, leap-frog, blindman's bluff and the timeless "odd man out" are shown. On looking at the painting recently, I noticed that even the three-year-old boys had enormous codpieces—a further mark of the adultness of children of that period.

As we arrive in the New World we find Chepa Rose, the "Narragansett Trunk Peddlar," was an important character in the life of children in colonial New England. He was an important communication link among the families of Rhode Island and Connecticut. He would set out every year with a full pack on his back. He carried books, tinker's tools, toys and household necessities. There being no inns along his rural routes, he would have to stay with his customers.

As the bearer of news he was always welcome and he exchanged news for room and board. During the evening after supper he would regale the children with toys, tricks and stories. Many hundreds of children over several generations learned from him. He was acknowledged to know more Indian lore than any other white man in Rhode Island. He taught the children Indian ways of survival, hunting and crafts. His skills with the jackknife were a legend and his wood carving was admired and copied by his hosts' children. It was a great day when Chepa Rose came through on his annual tour.

The Reverend John Pierpoint wrote:

> The Yankee Boy before he's sent to school
> Well knows the mysteries of that magic tool
> The pocket knife. To that his wistful eye
> Turns, while he hears his mother's lullaby.
> And in the education of the lad,
> No little part that implement hath had.
> His pocket knife to the young whittler brings,
> A growing knowledge of material things.
> Projectiles, music and the sculptor's art.
> His chestnut whistle, and his single dart
> His elder-pop-gin with its hickory rod
> Its sharp explosion and rebounding wad
> His corn stalk fiddle, and the deeper tone.

And on and on for a hundred more lines.

A comparative walk in any colonial and contemporary graveyard will prove how short was the life span of colonial children. Just a mile from my home there is a small graveyard dating from

Revolutionary times. There are more than twenty Kennedys interred there. More than half of the clan were under five years old when they met their Maker. Play was frequently a preparation for a short life.

Exactly two hundred years ago a girl wrote this verse on the first page of her copybook:

> The grass is green
> The rose is red
> Remember me
> When I am dead.

Johnathon Fell lived in New Hampshire before the Revolution. His cousin Abraham wrote to him from Philadelphia about schools and play.

"Our master tells us we must be 'quiet as a mouse and industrious as a beaver.'" Some of the rules Abe wrote about were: "In our hours of leisure, we shall avoid ranting games and diversions and quarreling with each other." The rich boys wore wigs and had to shave their heads daily. Both boys and girls dressed alike, then abruptly changed into adult clothing.

So it appears that the child's life in New England was almost all work and no play. Religion overshadowed all daily events. Their primers taught religious rhymes; they read from the Bible, the Catechism, the Psalm Book, and that lurid rhymed horror "The Day of Doom"; they parsed, too, from these universal books.

We have read that the children of New England were often subject to the harsh discipline of their puritanical parents. The following stories from the southern states indicate a much freer attitude towards life and especially to children.

Children from the Old Dominion State joined in with their parents in all sports and diversions. All sorts of activities were carried on which would have landed any Puritan in the stocks. Many games played by early Americans were adapted from the Indians. Lacrosse, described by visiting Englishman Basil Hall in 1828 while in Virginia, was one of these:

"One of the chiefs, having advanced to the centre of the arc, cast the ball high in the air. As it fell, between twenty and thirty players rushed forward and leaping several feet off the ground, tried to strike it. The multiplicity of blows, acting in different directions, had the effect of bringing the ball to the

1-4: Children have an inherent capacity to discover play possibilities. A playspace in London, England.

ground where a fine scramble took place. . . . At length an Indian, more expert than the others, contrived to nip the ball between the end of his two sticks and ran off with it like a deer, with his arms raised over his head pursued by a whole party engaged in the first struggle. The fortunate youth was, of course, intercepted in his progress twenty different times by his antagonists, who shot like hawks across his flight, from all parts of the field, to knock the prize out of his grasp, or to trip him up—in short by any means to prevent his throwing it through the opening between the boughs at the end of the playground. Whenever this grand purpose of the game was accomplished the successful party announced their right to count one by a fierce yell of triumph which pierced the very depths of the wilderness."

Before the Revolution, the status symbol for rich and doting parents in Philadelphia and Chester counties was "imported toys for children."

A Boston trading company was the Nieman-Marcus and F.A.O. Schwarz of colonial America. To have "toys from Boston" was to set the rich children above the others. The children's wigs often cost more than the year's wages of a common laborer. While wigs were made in America, only those fabricated in London had social significance.

While imported toys were at the top of the social ladder, the next rung was occupied by toys brought home by sailors. Very elaborate Chinese dolls were seen in many homes. While Japan was closed to trade in those days, almost every country was represented and known about by children due to ocean commerce of our Eastern cities.

Colonial children knew much about other countries, their children and their ways. In colonial days almost every family had one son who went to sea and traveled to China, the Middle East and all known parts of the world. They all brought back toys or made them during their leisure hours at sea.

Scrimshaw, whirligigs, cornstalk-stuffed dolls, whistles, tops and hundreds of other beautifully handmade toys were brought home.

Fortunately, almost all of these toys are now represented in our historical museums.

Just before the Revolution, the Philadelphia School Latin Newspaper was one of the first student publications in America. While it had adult guidance, it often went to press without censorship. This probably contributed to its short life span as a student paper. One issue took to task the students who:

1. Aped behind their master's back. (Ditto British soldiers, town officials and anyone representing authority).
2. Used fish hooks and lines connected through a hole in the ceiling. The fisherchild in the loft would then snag the wig of the rich child and haul it up to the ceiling, exposing the boy's bald pate to his classmates' derision.
3. Installed a full-sized wagon on the top of a high chimney so that the owner would then have to build a scaffold and dismantle it in order to rescue the wagon. Naturally the owner would have to perform this task with an audience of laughing children and adults.

One can read in today's paper how students put a professor's Volkswagen on the top of a hundred-foot-high water tank as a practical joke. Nothing has changed very much.

The first toy a boy had in colonial America was something he would carry to his grave—a jackknife of the highest quality.

1-5: Children use what they build.

With the jackknife a boy could whittle whistles, toys, wheels, tools, fire sticks, sculpture and play mumbly-peg. It and the gun were the toys and tools of survival.

As the boy's skill with the jackknife improved, his father would charge him to make items of necessity for the farm and the home. He soon learned to carve bowls, spoons, birch brooms and many of the utensils of the house. For the farm, he was set to first carving pegs, then simple tool handles and then the farm implements such as wagon spokes, rakes, plows, etc. Most farmsteads had a jack-draw bench which was used to hold pieces of wood on which work was done.

The two low points of children's play in America were during the latter part of the nineteenth century, when very few children had time to play, and the present, when very few children know how to play. In the late nineteenth century, sweat shops often took up the child's time. The eight-year-old often worked a sixteen-hour day, seven days a week. While the pay was small, the child's main contribution to the house was that he was not a drain on his parents.

In a child-worked New England mill, there was a sign which stated: "Don't Waste The Time Of This Machine, Your Value Is Gauged By What You Can Get Out Of This Machine. Keep It At Top Speed."

Play Today

Often the problem was to choose between the lesser of two evils. Many children actually chose work in the mill or mine in preference to going to school, being beaten by the teacher, learning nothing and being abused at home for being a parasite. At least one could bring home a pay envelope and contribute to the family.

The child is no longer the slave of the mill owner. Our children have replaced the mill owner with TV, junk food emporia and blocks of concrete objects called playgrounds. The child is not left alone to develop at a normal rate. The boy is bombarded with commercial doubts about his masculinity as much as the girl is questioned about her femininity. Buy this, visit fantasy land, try a new breakfast cereal that not only barks but makes you more attractive to the opposite sex, wear the latest fad, play the latest record, hang out at this week's "in" spot.

Fifty years ago, the children in the six one-room schoolhouses of my home township, Charlestown, played in the mud and snow and enjoyed the elements and each other. Now, with a new million-dollar school complete with terrazzo floors, the children are not allowed out to play in the snow. They spend several hours a day on a school bus and are taught more by machines than humans.

Their playgrounds are static and sterile. There are no rope or tire swings. The manufactured swings are broken. The architect told us the terrazzo floor would be impervious to snow, mud or water. But the janitor doesn't want to do his job and mop the floor, so 350 country kids can't build snow forts or men or slide or skate. They go home and terrorize their parents with their pent-up energy.

Today there is neither time nor space in the child's world for tree houses, caves, mud puddles and such. There are no more mud puddles. All is asphalt. The tree house has been replaced by a $5,000 prefabricated steel pipe rocket ship which challenges the child's imagination in two ways. The first challenge which appears in the four-color catalogue is to help the child imagine he is an astronaut. This challenge lasts up to fifteen minutes.

The greater challenge is to see how to take the rocket ship apart. This might take up to a full work-week for ten children. I can't believe our recreation leaders don't see this. I can only conclude that they have too great an investment to back off now and redirect their energies and our money to service rather than product.

A recent study told of playground accessibility in Czechoslovakia. A child who lives on the twentieth floor of a Prague housing complex generally has greater mental problems than one who lives on the tenth floor, who in turn has more than the child living on the first floor. Distance from a playground was proved to be an important determining factor in the child's mental health. The further the child was from a playsite, the more he was the victim of mental disorders.

Back in 1928, the Required Plan Association of New York, in a report which remains to this day the most exhaustive American study of big-city recreation, had this to say:

"Careful checking within a radius of ¼ mile of playgrounds under a wide range of conditions in many cities showed that about 1/7 of the child population from 5 to 15 years of age may be found on these grounds—the lure of the street is a strong competitor—it must be a well-administered playground to successfully compete with the city streets, teeming with life and adventure. The ability to make the playground activity so compellingly attractive as to draw the children from the streets and hold their interest from day to day is a rare faculty in play leadership, combining personality and technical skill of a high order."

In America today, children's play is at its lowest point in history. The basic elements of life—fire, water, food and shelter—are no longer a part of the scene in our playgrounds. Play is directed from above (adults) and scorned. Our playgrounds are designed by adults and destroyed by children.

1-6: Children building their own playground at the Roosevelt Elementary School, Hanford, California. The outer perimeter defense is made up of poles donated by the electric company.

1-7: The main gate of Fort Roosevelt, which the children elected to put on rollers.

1-8

1-9

1-8 through 1-12: If there's a choice between an elaborate playground and a natural setting, children will likely choose the latter. This playground in Central Park is fortunate to have both.

1-10

1-11

1-12

The theme of a recent Michigan Park & Recreation Association meeting held last year in Lansing was "Security in the Playground." My partner, Bill Gohdes, attended the conference and told me it was dominated by manufacturers of closed circuit TV cameras, fence builders, concrete turtle makers and the like. When he mentioned that we had built two hundred playgrounds on a community volunteer basis and experienced no vandalism, he was laughed at.

In Europe today they are progressing towards the high point of free play and the adventure playground. At this moment there are more than two hundred adventure playgrounds in England. There are less than ten part-time ones in America.

The rest of the world is somewhere in between Europe and America. That hopefully will be their salvation. If they can avoid the pitfalls of the big-money American playgrounds and develop people-oriented playgrounds along the advanced lines of the European free playgrounds, they will save themselves a lot of heartaches.

If we can no longer follow Zachariah and have the streets full of playing boys and girls, can't we at least provide attractive and inviting alternatives, places where our children can grow, learn, play, create and be free?

Play at Home

To paraphrase "charity begins at home," perhaps I can say "play begins at home." A child who is nurtured from his first days with a parental attitude which promotes free play and adventure is well on his way towards a creative and joyful life.

The balance of freedom with security is no less important to the child than it is to the nation. Achieving that balance, like the yin and yang, is a delicate matter. It needs constant attention. The parent must "enable" the child to play.

The child must be free to put a sheet over the dining room table on a rainy day and create his own living environment. If the parent forbids such creative play, the child will suffer. If the parent forbids the child from digging up the yard, building a shanty or a tree house, constructing a soapbox racer, operating a lemonade stand, having club meetings in the basement or attic, then the child, and the parent as well, will suffer.

While the child must have this freedom to grow he must have the security which parental guidelines should offer. The young girl must be allowed to play with fire but be made to understand both the threat and benefits of fire. We live in the country and burn our paper trash. We always allow the children the privilege of burning the trash. They are eager to do this chore—almost as eager as when participating in the semiannual burning of old, dead branches, litter thrown on our road, and other junk which appears as if by magic.

What is the parent's stake in the child's play? Simply put, the same as the parent's stake in clothing, feeding, housing and educating the child. Play is an integral part of the growth process. Lacking it, the child will forever have a void in his life. A parent should no more ignore the play needs of the child than the hunger pangs of the child. The parent's stake is a happy, well-rounded and fulfilled child.

Equally important, an awareness of the play needs of children can help keep us all playful and spontaneous throughout our lives. To dance with our children is to dance for life.

How can the parent bring about an atmosphere of play and learning? The most important tool to nurture a child is the proper attitude—a willingness to allow the child to get dirty, dig holes in the backyard, if not the front. The parent must use a mental time-machine to go back to his own childhood. If the parent got by on a homemade soapbox racer, where is the need to give the child a battery-powered fiberglass car?

The parent must supply tools, time, space and attitude for the child to draw on. Like a prompter in that little hidden box on the opera stage, the parent must not interfere but be available when needed—when lines are forgotten, or skills need developing or precautions must be offered.

We sometimes put the red three-bladed propeller sign of radioactivity on our children's bedroom door. We joke that it is a contaminated area, but we know that it is really a place of freedom and security for the child. It is a place where the child is master of his or her environment, however contaminated it may be to our eyes. Yet, the child's bedroom is still an important part of the house and there is security for the child in that knowledge.

The backyard and the corner lot should be set aside for the child as a growth extension of the child's maturation.

My childhood backyard had dirt and flowers along with all the children of the neighborhood. We coexisted. I go back to the house where I was born every few years. There is still dirt and flowers in the yard and all the neighborhood kids are playing and building and growing.

The children are banging 2 x 4s together, planting a garden, rebuilding their tree house for the hundredth time in fifty years. There is no need to say "let me hammer."

Community Play

Recently I directed the construction of a half dozen playgrounds in various neighborhoods of Newark, New Jersey. We were sponsored by the Trust For Public Land, a San Francisco-based foundation devoted to rural and urban land acquisition for open space preservation.

Some of the Newark communities had been asking for playgrounds for six or seven years. TPL joined with them to help each organization to construct the play facility. The city cleared and cleaned up the site and lent a backhoe when needed. TPL provided a few hundred dollars worth of material. Playground Clearing House provided the tools and supervision and the community provided the labor.

At each of the six sites we would show up at 9:00 a.m. on a Saturday. More often than not we'd be alone and my hopes would be dashed. Within minutes the kids would pop out and by 10:00 a.m. a dozen fathers would turn out to help with the work.

Although I have directed the construction of more than 250 play environments, there has never been a set pattern. Newark was no exception. Sometimes the most qualified man would be content to dig ditches. The least qualified wanted to be boss. Sullen teenagers would scorn our work, but by late morning would be hammering and sawing and lifting heavy utility poles.

Soon the refreshments would arrive and a luncheon banquet would be served that would put us out of action for an hour. By 2:00 p.m. the entire community would be a smooth-running crew. People would both give and follow orders. If a child got out of line an adult, not necessarily the parent, would correct him in a kindly parental way. It was a beautiful example of the extended family where all parents are responsible for all children —not just their own.

The biggest problem I faced with the children was their ignorance of tools and their proper usage. Too often I'd see a young builder using a good wood saw to cut a steel pipe or a hacksaw to saw a pole or a sharp hatchet to break up concrete.

If there are no backyards to hammer and build in, the school system or the city should provide the opportunity for these children to grow and learn. The system should "enable" the children to play/work.

On only one of the six playgrounds did I have trouble. I point this out merely to show that building playspaces in the real world can be made a lot easier when the "space" grows from within a community.

It was a Monday. We hadn't finished on Saturday and were working with a few children and adults to finish up the project.

Two twelve-year-old boys began to annoy me by banging on my truck with a wrench. They wouldn't stop when I asked so I took the wrenches away. They got other things to bang with and I got more and more uptight. I told them to bang each other if they wanted to bang something and they responded that they would rather bang me or my truck.

I asked them, "Do you want me to finish this playground or do you want me to leave?" "Makes no difference to me, man, because we're going to wreck it as soon as you leave," was their reply.

I immediately stopped work and put all my tools in the truck. I told them, "I never go where I'm not wanted and it won't affect me if you tear this place apart—but it will affect your kid brothers and sisters, so just go ahead and the little kids can go back to playing in the streets."

Just then one of the block captains came up and asked for an explanation. I told her that I never went where I wasn't wanted. She naturally exploded and collared the two youths and gave them a dressing-down that would have withered a concrete turtle. The upshot was that the youths joined in, we became working partners, and the playground still stands. You never know.

The one universal reaction to these "playground raising" days is the parents' awareness of the parent/child role in work-

1-13: Children at the Lincoln
School installing a tire walk.
(Courtesy of Florence H. Trallee)

1-14: Bill Gohdes of Playground Clearing House is shown laying
out the detail work for parents at the Lincoln Elementary School,
Pompton Lakes, New Jersey.
(Courtesy of Florence H. Trallee)

1-15: Paul Hogan (second from left) and Bill Gohdes (far right) constructing a tire pyramid with fathers at the Lincoln School.
(Courtesy of Florence H. Trallee)

ing/playing together. Whether it is Newark or Larchmont, the afterglow is the same. The father's giving up a date with the television or the mother's forgoing of a meeting to join the extended family in building a playground has had long-lasting effects.

The parents, by working closely with their children, learn that their children have basic skills which must be nurtured and developed. They learn that children must by nature copy their parents. If there is no father or mother in the home, the father of the extended neighborhood family must show the son how to spear the lion or build a house. The female adult must teach the new skills as well as the old to the girls in the house or the community.

The request most asked of me by children is "let me hammer." We must let the children hammer. So many hundreds of times I've seen adults take hammers from children's hands to do the work for them. I should record the look of disappointment and frustration in a child's eyes when an adult shows off his superior skill at hammering.

The Evolution of a Playground

Like most other schools in America, the Randall Elementary School, 1802 Regent Street, Madison, Wisconsin (53705), had a blacktopped play surface. There was an obvious need for change.

Carol Grogan and Jane Wanamaker, co-chairpersons for the playground project, got busy and inventoried the resources of the community. In the fall of 1973, following a slide presentation and discussion by Don Brault, Coordinator for Physical Education for the Metropolitan Madison School District, the Randall School PTA formed a playground development committee.

Early in the process it was decided that all ages would be welcome during and after school hours. Two sites on the school grounds were chosen. One site was the large open blacktopped area behind the school and the other area was a small enclosed courtyard space between two wings of the school.

At all stages of the process, input was received from the children. The final design was aided by the Design Coalition of Madison, the departments of Recreation and Buildings and Grounds of the Madison public school system. The total cost of the project was $8,000. For the first phase more than $2,000 was spent in removing the asphalt, installing a storm drain and returning the site to its original state. Railroad ties, which were used to hold back the tree bark surfacing material, cost $600 and $20 was spent on tool rental for the construction day. More than two thousand labor hours were donated by the parents, friends and neighbors of the school. The second and third phase saw the introduction of massive timbers, tires, hardware and special equipment. The recreation department of the school district estimated the value of the work at $30,000.

A recent follow-up letter from Don Brault tells me: "At those schools where children, parents and teachers have been involved in planning and building new play environments, vandalism is almost zero. The preponderance of accidents on elementary school playgrounds occurs in those areas normally assumed to be safest, namely the blacktop and grass play fields. Our wooden play structures and those made of tires have a surprisingly low accident rate when viewed in terms of the number of children play-hours. Also our experience indicates that accidents on these types of play structures generally occur within the first two weeks of use and practically disappear after that time."

Some time after the construction of the playground, Don Brault told me that the vandalism, truancy and other negative factors were far below average in those schools which had playgrounds built by the children and which were thus more open to new play and recreation ideas.

Planning for Play

I've spoken to perhaps a thousand audiences about playgrounds during the past ten years. I receive all sorts of questions, but each group presents at least one "why don't you build someplace else" and one "I just don't see how we can get started."

I give short shrift to the nay-sayer, but try to explain to the one who sincerely wants to start but doesn't quite know how.

It doesn't really matter if you are going to build a model airplane, a piece of play equipment for your backyard, a large community playground or a twenty-story office building.

You must first take an inventory of your assets and liabilities. My basic advice is to think small—small is beautiful. You must

1-16: The Randall School playground (Madison, Wisconsin) before construction.
(Courtesy of C. Grogan)

1-17: Parents meet at the model design session to plan for future construction of the playground at the Randall School.
(Courtesy of C. Grogan)

1-18: A view of the interior court of the Randall School.
(Courtesy of C. Grogan)

1-19: An "after" view of the Randall School playground.
(Courtesy of C. Grogan)

know your skills, tools, materials or lack of these. Try to fit the project into your "have" column and ignore the "have not" side of your resources.

If you can get some 2 x 4s, have a hammer and saw and some apprentice carpentry skills, then start from there. Obtain a plan from Playgrounds For Free (26 Buckwalter Road, Phoenix-ville, Pa. 19460), or any do-it-yourself publication. If you can't obtain a plan, draw one up yourself. It doesn't have to be professional—just so you can get a visual feeling for the construction.

Look around your community; there's always tires, railroad ties, and similar material to be found.

If it's a community playground, then your skills, materials and tools can take a multiple of ten. Take an inventory of your collective skills, collective materials, collective tools and apportion the work accordingly.

If it is a small or large operation, try to set as a goal one thing to be totally completed in one day. It is discouraging to leave a job unfinished. It always rains the next day and the following week your star carpenter has to visit his in-laws.

This might be a good time schedule:
1. Meet with a few very interested people and arrange
2. a larger meeting with representatives from all factions—especially the children. Then
3. elect a permanent chairperson to organize the committee and appoint subcommittee chairpeople.

You should have a committee for:
a. design
b. publicity
c. inventory
d. refreshments
e. safety
f. political coordination

Design is important and should meet the needs of the children, the materials at hand and the abilities of the workers.

Publicity is necessary to recruit workers, raise funds, obtain material donations, win approval of the nay-sayers and create a feeling of community involvement.

Inventory is just that—knowing what resources are available.

Workers can't work on empty stomachs and they need constant refreshment plus a good lunch. Brown-bagging it is OK—but a potluck luncheon is much better for morale.

Health and safety precautions are vital. Know the best way to the hospital, have first aid available and one or two safety officers whose only job is to watch others. Use ear protectors for chain saw work and safety glasses, hard hats, heavy gloves and shoes. No sneakers allowed and high heels, open-toed shoes and loafers should not be allowed on the job site. Make this known well in advance and don't be afraid to send people home or have them sign a release.

Political coordination might sound like a strange committee job, but it is easy to step on toes if you don't cover all bases. Keep the local recreation director informed so he doesn't read in the newspaper that he suddenly has a new playground in his domain. If you are going to depend on the politicians to get your grass cut or your trash picked up, keep in touch with them. They are also human and like to know what is going on. We always depend on the politicians to get us a township bulldozer or borough dump truck.

And finally, it's good to have a party when the job is done. A keg of beer or a barrel of cider, hot dogs, music, give the workers a vote of appreciation and a feeling that it was worth all the trouble.

Recently I worked on my second playground in Baltimore. We had several paid summer Job Corps youths working there. One young man fixed my generator on his own time—something professional mechanics couldn't do at $20 per hour. He had had two previous summer jobs—one raking leaves for an hour a day and playing cards the other seven. His other job was as a watchman at a golf course where he was paid to play cards eight hours a day.

A week after his paid work was terminated, he still came around to offer his services. He told me, "You know, I like to work, this work means something. I never really knew what work was. I thought it was a joke where you go someplace to play cards and they paid you to stay out of trouble. This work is like play to me and I want to keep on working. Can I have a job with you?"

This experience is not totally unique. It has been my impression over the years that those people who have been involved in planning and constructing community playspaces have left the project with healthier attitudes toward play and recreation.

As you will learn in subsequent chapters, involvement in the recreation activities of a community represents a commitment to home, family, and—well, history. It represents a commitment to children who, as Abraham Lincoln notes in the following passage, will be playing with our future.

"A child is a person who is going to carry on what you have started. He is going to sit where you are sitting, and when you are gone, attend to those things which you think are important. You may adopt all the policies you please, but how they are carried out depends on him. He will assume control of your cities, states, and nations. He is going to move in and take over your churches, schools, universities, and corporations . . . the fate of humanity is in his hands."

chapter 2

The Cycle

by James C. McCullagh

Recycling is in fashion. Manure becomes delicate tomatoes; sludge, the topsoil of the earth. Bottles are refilled and reused. Cans, picked up, pressed, and recast, find their way back to the grocery shelf. Tires are on retreads.

Kitchen wastes fill the black hole of the compost pit bringing new life and energy to next year's crop. The cycle is completed; dust to dust, humus to humus, cabbage leaves to cabbage heads.

Recycling is the highest organic announcement, the ultimate activity. Garbage is transformed into new delights. Trash heaps and junk piles diminish, as if from within.

Theoretically, at least, it is relatively easy to recycle the landscape. What is difficult is to recycle our attitudes toward the landscape, to look beyond a "dead fish of an eyesore" to a new park, a green space, a playground. Most frequently, it is a matter of recycling our attitudes and perceptions toward molested space. Anyone living in the heart of New York or Los Angeles or in thousands of small towns and cities might understand what W. H. Auden meant when he called for "new styles of architecture, a change of heart." More than most people of this century, Auden saw that the recycling of physical structures was tied to a change in our perception of things. One could not be changed without the other.

What, you might be asking yourself, does the question of recycling have to do with and in a book about play? Indeed, how do you recycle for play?

First of all, it is going to become increasingly difficult for us, in this age of shrinking land and diminishing natural re-

31

2-1: While this tire structure is the heaviest piece of equipment in the playground, usually a phone call will bring the tire dealer running.
(Courtesy of *Minneapolis Star*)

sources, to separate the playing from the space which holds the play.

And secondly, there are numerous ways to recycle for play. You might follow the wrecking crew from a telephone company that is replacing useable old poles. Most of the time the crews simply deposit the poles by the wayside for the "recycler's" benefit. With a little ingenuity (and sleight of hand) these telephone poles might find their way into a playground in your community. And what about the piles of old tires commonly found at the city dump?

Paul Hogan, who probably knows more about recycling materials for play than anyone, has found use for cable reels, tanks and drums, concrete pipes, utility poles, railroad ties, tires, inner tubes, etc., in his construction of hundreds of community playspaces.

There are, of course, higher mountains to cross and deeper eyesores to eliminate. Perhaps, in a very fundamental way, recycling for play means that we take a new and daring look at our environment and community, and recognize that as new spaces become more difficult to find, old spaces will have to be seen in a new light. That, instead of traveling to Europe, we will find our recreation at home. That, like children, we will find our play in some unlikely spots.

And as you will discover in this chapter, a great deal of this kind of activity is going on in communities throughout the country, more often than not led by individuals who believe that, out of nothing, can come play and recreation; by individuals who believe (and have demonstrated) that the average citizen can bring about changes in the towns and cities of this nation.

Allegory from the Grave

The scene opens as naturally as a green afternoon. The children are playing in a crowded playground in New York. The swings, the slides, and the seesaws are put on the children's waiting list: they are something to be lined up for.

The children get restless and begin to push out beyond the playground into a nearby cemetery. Before long, the kids are dancing on top of graves, meaning absolutely no disrespect. They have spilled over into play; their play has spilled over into a holy place customarily considered off-limits. The "spilling-over" is not premeditated. Kids, when doing the jig or playing marbles, need elbow room; like water, they will find the cavity—and fill it with their jubilation.

The above story forcefully dramatizes, in somewhat exotic terms, a universal need to play, which is evident particularly in children. To play, to move the body through its circuit, demands space, breathing room, a place to giggle and dance.

Unfortunately, all too often play is crowded out of our imaginations; green land is gobbled up in a fit of progress; parks are cast in the shadows of office buildings and vast highway networks.

If, on the one hand, recreation space is being gobbled up, on the other, traditional recreation spaces are becoming more difficult to reach.

According to Seymour Gold writing in *Parks and Recreation,* "The existing system of recreation spaces will be all most communities can afford to maintain. Funds will not be available for new spaces, which suggests making the best use of existing spaces that desperately need renewal.

"The traditional priorities of land acquisition, development, and programs are being reversed in some cities that are beginning to sense the city as a recreation place in which voluntary program leadership is more effective than existing investments in land and facilities."

Evanston, Illinois

Some of these factors have forced communities to re-examine themselves, to consider even some of the most unlikely areas as play and recreation sites. Take Mount Trashmore, for instance, a recycled ski hill in Evanston, Illinois. According to resident Bob McCray, "It was once one end of the city dump. The hill was made of hunks of concrete, clay, dirt, and other inorganic garbage. That's how it got its name, 'Mt. Trashmore.'"

The hill was sodded over, the slopes lined with clusters of evergreens, and sculpted into a picturesque "Rocky," which rises modestly against the Chicago skyline. Now it stands as Evanston's contribution to a total winter sports program, including skiing, tobogganing, cross-country skiing and skating.

A winter sundown over Evanston's own "rocky mountain" isn't quite like Aspen, Colorado. After all, the vertical drop is only sixty-five feet, and the snow is not deep or powdery. Nevertheless, drop by any winter weekend and you'll find the skiing as intense, parkas as bright, the latest parallel techniques, hotdogging, and all the joy that goes with the great outdoor sport of skiing.

All this did not happen overnight. Actually, it all began back in 1942, when the city of Evanston purchased the land. Originally, the forty-eight or so acres was a clay pit—eighty feet deep —used by a local brick company.

The city bought the land and rented it to private scavengers. For approximately ten years, the pit was used as a dump. Fill included trash of most types except garbage and trees infected with Dutch elm disease. Throughout the period of filling there were no legal restrictions against burning. All trash was burned first, then compressed and tamped down by heavy machinery. Burning was limited so as not to create problems with the surrounding community. Certain materials, such as huge tree stumps which could not be completely burned and would create air pockets in the landfill, were not allowed. Items that had air pockets, such as tin cans, were allowed if they could be completely compressed by heavy equipment so no air pockets would remain.

In 1953, the city began using the area for its own trash disposal, subject again to regulations as to types of fill.

Once the pit was filled to ground level, the building of the hill began. For the hill only very heavy materials were used, such as cement slabs from buildings that had been razed, or concrete from torn-up streets and curbs. Contractors hired by the city to put in streets and curbs much preferred dumping concrete nearby to hauling it fifteen miles away and having to pay a fee to dump.

Shaping and topping the hill was done by two city bulldozers. The last dumping was done in 1965, and the first use of the hill as a toboggan hill was in the winter of 1967.

Since then the hill has been improved each year, and in 1974 it was prepared for skiing. A rope tow was installed, along with lights for night skiing. Snowmaking equipment was installed to extend the season by six weeks.

The first year in use as a multiple-use winter sports area, Mt. Trashmore accommodated over fourteen thousand skiers, sledders and tobogganers.

Vito De Canio, Superintendent of Parks in Evanston, has been in charge of the maintenance of Mt. Trashmore since 1972. He is the one who usually answers inquiries from neighboring towns on the recycled hill.

He says, "To build a fifty-, sixty-, or seventy-foot hill you need a good solid foundation.

"Concrete and clay are good fillers," he says, "We frequently get calls from contractors who offer to dump concrete and clay free, for a 'short haul.' In fact, sometimes they'll even throw in free bulldozing to move it up the hill.

"On the other hand, sand is not a good fill. Pure sand percolates. With pure sand, water goes through and it will wash out," says Mr. De Canio.

2-2

2-2 through 2-5: Recycling for play in Evanston, Illinois.
(Courtesy of Bob McCray)

2-3

2-4

2-5

"And dirt gets expensive. I'd 'guestimate' that it would take thousands of yards of dirt to build our hill. At five or six dollars a yard that's a lot of money," he says.

"So far there haven't been any problems with Mount Trashmore," says De Canio. "We did it on our own, without any model plan, so to speak. So far it has worked out well, with only a few problems. For example, we tried to seed the hill to get grass. But it would rain and wash out the seed. We put down sod then, on the north side—the side intended for skiing and sledding. On the rest of the hill we used groundcover. It spread well, choking out the weeds, and is a beautiful green color.

"Another thing we didn't plan on was the strong wind that blew on the top of our sixty-foot hill. We had to install a six-foot windbreak fence so people wouldn't freeze up there," he says.

"And of course there are yearly maintenance problems. When sledding is allowed during warm weather, the turf balls up. In the summer, children wear paths on the hill. And, the snow-making equipment lays heavy on the trees, and has killed a few. But all in all the hill has worked out well, and we've had no big problems."

So far there are no ski condominiums springing up around Evanston, and the local recreation director can't foresee the day when the Olympic downhill tryouts will be held on the slopes. On the other hand, Mt. Trashmore does offer reasonably priced skiing. It's a good place to loosen up and get some practice, or try out new gear. And it makes family recreation available, nearby, to a large number of people.

Is it any wonder that Evanstonians are proud of their hill, and support their recycled hill with "Ski Evanston" bumper stickers?

And what do "Trashmores" have to do with recreation and play? Plenty. At least, the Mt. Trashmore in Illinois—which is a fine example of a community taking charge of its own recreation, of a community which gives the science of recycling an aesthetic dimension. This is a community that found recreation in its own backyard.

But the nation is full of creative and forward-looking communities which have, for example, found play where another might see an expressway ramp. How much imagination did it take for the planners to incorporate an all-weather basketball court under a highway ramp in Eugene, Oregon? The needs of the motorists and the needs of the players are met.

And consider the accompanying photographs of parks, playgrounds, and informal rest areas on top of parking lots in San Francisco. In existence for the last twenty years, these have become landmarks, and are regarded as part of the scenery. A place in the heart of the city where both young and old can—together or separately—find solace and play. No wonder one woman described her "park" visit as the high point in her day. (Interestingly, Sweden is already considering how to recycle parking garages when the automobile population in the country declines.)

But recycling the community for play is not just an urban phenomenon; it can happen everywhere. In fact, more and more communities, more and more individuals are beginning to realize that taking part in community recreation planning is as important as voting. It becomes, as some have explained, in and of itself, "a kind of recreation." In other words, getting involved with community organizations to turn an eyesore into a playspace represents a form of recreation—in the best sense. People, with their own energies, "re-create" a space and, in turn, "re-create" themselves in some significant way.

Miamisburg, Ohio

Take the city of Miamisburg, Ohio, for example. In announcing a successful "recycling" project the recreation directors wrote, "The Ugly Duckling has hatched into a beautiful Swan. Yes, the old abandoned sewage treatment plant in Miamisburg is now an attractive neighborhood park."

Charles E. Dressler and Robert Jewell report in *The American City* that "we 'found' a six-acre park. Our discovery was an abandoned sewage treatment plant which had become an embarrassing eyesore.

"Once the residents of the moderate-income housing development surrounding the plant had complained about the odor. Then they complained about the unused plant creating a neighborhood nuisance.

"Population and demand called for a park-type facility in the area. The closest open space was an undeveloped field one mile away. Converting the abandoned plant into a park would not

2-7

2-6 *through* 2-11: Playspaces
above parking lots in San
Francisco, California.

2-6

2-8

2-9

2-10

2-11

2-12: Basketball facilities under highway ramp in Eugene, Oregon.

2-13: Close-up, basketball courts.

only eliminate the eyesore, but create a much-needed recreational area."

The local paper gave strong support to the project as did the city council. Importantly, the opportunity for citizen participation was great. Nearly three hundred homeowners were asked for their ideas about the proposed park. Of these, ninety-eight responded and twenty-eight of these volunteered to serve on the neighborhood advisory council to assist in the project.

The people of the neighborhood decided that the most important facilities for the space were a tot-lot, a wading pool, a roller skating area, a creative play area, a basketball-tennis complex, a baseball-softball diamond, horseshoe course, and open space for informal play.

In the interest of economics the people decided to make use of as many of the existing structures as possible. Accordingly, sludge beds are being converted into areas for basketball, volleyball, stick-hockey, and a regulation tennis court. The aeroclarifier will serve as a wading pool and a roller skating area. The digester will become an adventure playground for the younger boys and girls. In other words, the site was grandly recycled for play.

Dressler and Jewell report that "traditional play apparatus received only minimal priority. Instead, the playground design provides an opportunity for multipurpose uses within a limited area.

"When the sewage treatment plant was abandoned, neighborhood children were attracted to the digester. This mound is 235 feet in circumference with a 25-foot slope. The building has steps, pits and pipes.

"The children actually dug under and climbed over the fence to get at this area, not as vandals but as curious youngsters trying to satisfy an element of adventure. Therefore, it was felt that the area should be preserved and designed in such a way as to remove the dangerous objects.

"The equipment that will be placed in this area is of the type that provides swinging, sliding and balancing opportunities. It will be designed in such a way as to avoid a single pattern of play and learning experience.

"To make the digester a functional play facility, an earthen ramp was built along and up one side. Over fifty tons of scrap steel will be removed, the open pit will be filled with dirt and concrete will be removed from the sludge beds.

"The earth used for the ramp will be bulldozed into the aero-clarifier. Each of these two structures will be capped with rubberized asphalt allowing for a soft play surface.

"The adventure area will employ the link play concept. In other words, it will provide experiences ranging from the very simple to the complex.

"Traditional play apparatus such as standard swings or slides does not permit spontaneous play. The various elements of the adventure area will consist of sliding, swinging, climbing, jumping and balancing through a scale to which all children can relate.

"In addition, a tot-lot, complete with logs, swing sets, sand box, tile and seating area, has been included for pre-schoolers. This area will be fenced off and screened with plantings to keep the tots inside and the animals out."

2-14: Playground on top of digester, Miamisburg, Ohio.

Seattle, Washington

But just how much one community cycles or recycles depends on the imagination of its citizens. Recycling often means rethinking, relooking at an eyesore and discovering a thing of beauty; it is the magician's trick; turning a sow's ear into a silk purse. Such is the case of the Seattle Gas Works, which to some represented "a neo-Gothic nightmare of industrial blight" which should be torn down. But, to others, "the gas works is not an eyesore, but a thing of beauty—a rough, gutty thing," says architect Fred Bassetti, "a tentacular form like an animal exposed, a vitality that can't be imposed on."

Kenneth E. Read, writing in *Seattle Magazine,* compared visiting the gas works to visiting other celebrated ancient ruins. "There is no need," he writes, "to go to Europe or to suffer the rigors of the Yucatán in order to find the peculiar, yearning urgency of ruins. You can do it just as well, and far more comfortably, from the window-table in the bar of The Hungry Turtle, located at the foot of East Roanoke on the shore of Lake Union.

"The best time for the pilgrimage is a summer evening close to sunset, though fall and winter, cloudy days with rain or snow, add their particular measure to the ambience. Go there when the sun is low, for you will have to look toward the source of light. As the surface of the lake starts its nightly celebration, it is flushed with green and coppery gold. The sky is as wide and frail as the echoing vibration from a plucked string. Household lights are watch-fires on the hills. And there, on the northern shore, is the ruin you have come to see."

All this about a gas works which has been recycled into a playspace? Yes, and there is more.

"The gas works," Read continues, "can mean any number of things. I suspect that city-planners and Sunday sailors regard it as a prime example of urban blight, a superannuated industrial plant occupying a site best given to a high-rise condominium or a neat little inner-city park with redwood tables and judiciously spaced water spigots. But it is also a primer in the vision of nature that led to cubism. The essential forms are all there: planes and cylinders, cones and spheres balanced one against another in the manner of Cézanne or the popularized, latter-day

2-15 through 2-18: In Seattle, Washington, out of nothing, comes play.

2-15

2-16

2-17

2-18

economy of Buffet, whose spare style seems to have, unfortunately, a special appeal to decorators of motel chains.

"But go farther back, and here is Hieronymus Bosch alive and well in Seattle, limning his strange phantasies of the psyche and the flesh. The dark frames of stanchions and roof-lines enclose a lurid vision of apocalypse, in which quasi-human figures couple and destroy themselves while death and pestilence, war and vaulting ambition are seen as mounted skeletons riding a cosmic wind. With some stretch of the imagination (and a third martini) one can hear the squeaky voices of creatures engaged in flagellations and visceral orgies in the rank summer-growth of grasses. And Rousseau, *le Douanier,* is here as well. His lemon-eyed lions own these wastes of bull-rush and water-parsley, convolvulus and thorn. Even Dürer may have sat at the margin of the water and carefully etched the tender filaments of roots searching for nourishment in the despised mud.

"But if the distant view does not attract you, go there during the day. Don't worry that your way is blocked, that the whole edifice is cordoned by a high wire fence and there are no caretakers to admit you, reluctantly, at the ringing of a bell. Climb the wire fence and add the heady feeling of trespass to the experience of silence and desertion. This is when the ghosts walk and you feel them with you in the northern light that hangs the snow-flake forms of spiderwebs against the flying buttresses of concrete stairs, and unused corridors diminish in the echoing perspectives of a Gothic novel."

But above everything else the Seattle Gas Works is a park, perhaps the only one in the world which has been made of recycled junk. A type of playspace that conforms crudely but beautifully to Seattle's skyline.

The Gas Works Park is a place for "people of all ages," reports Hugh Roberston in *View Northwest.* "Children, gleeful and whooping, romp, rollick, scoot, scamper and climb through, over and around wildly painted great chunks of machinery which once helped make the gas that lighted Seattle's streets.

"There are motors in magenta and cerise, and giant gears which no longer grind or grumble, but stand fireman's red and ready for clambering, and long lavender pipes to be saddled and straddled. All this color and climbing is in the park's 'playbarn,' a recycled structure which once was what the engineers called an 'exhauster house.' When you watch children joyfully working through it you wonder why they changed the name.

"Right beside the exhauster/playbarn there's a once-was boiler house converted now for picnic cookery, with a fireplace and barbecues and tables and benches and sinks. There's also been a loft built in as a platform for impromptu performers.

"Outside, there's a soft sweeping hillside, grass-woven and glistening in the slanting sun. Down across the long length of Lake Union there's the rowing skyline of downtown Seattle, and if your timing's right, you can see sunset framed by giant rusting Tinker Toys. There's more space and light at the Gas Works Park than anywhere else in the city.

"There are no trees, no shaded walks. It's not a strolling park; it's a sprawl-in-the-sun park, a lie-on-your-back-and-look-at-the-sky park. It's a place for dogs to run and people to walk, a place to sail kites in crisp winds, a place to watch gulls wheel and swoop, a place to sense the city around you."

The park is used by all—often you can see two or three generations at one time playing in this space. Richard Haag, the architect of the project, knows of "one particular sixty-seven-year-old man who climbs the rafters with the children. I often see grandmothers on top of these mounds with their grandchildren."

Los Angeles County, California

Clearly, the Seattle Gas Works Park is an aesthetic delight, a joy to the Northwest. Perhaps what is not so clear is that a recycled space of this magnitude can be brought into being by an individual who believes in community recreation spaces. Consider, for example, Mrs. Frances Young and the South Coast Botanic Garden.

Take an eighty-seven-acre hole, fill it with 3½ million tons of trash, and what have you got? Trouble? Not if you think of it like Mrs. Young did. She forcibly led local government administrators into creating a unique botanic garden. A botanic garden that has pioneered the way for other problem sites to be made useful.

At that time, in 1958, Frances was "past sixty" and just back from a trip to the nearest arboretum. During the normally one-and-a-half-hour drive she was caught in a four-hour-long traffic

2-19: Mrs. Young chats with visitors to the botanic garden.
(Courtesy of Mark Wall)

jam. According to Frances, she spent the night "in frustration." She immediately proceeded to collect two thousand signatures from local garden and horticultural society members to show the number of taxpayers that were interested in a local botanic garden.

Mrs. Young also presented the idea to all nearby cities and received initial approval. The county quickly explained that no property was available for a botanic garden. But Frances knew of an old diatomaceous earth mine, five minutes' drive away, that had recently been purchased as a landfill site by the county.

That site was mentioned in the petition, along with the tentative approval given by all nearby cities. It was then turned over to the Board of Supervisors—the top administrative authority in the county—"rather than risk the possible shelving of the information by the Sanitation Department," according to Mrs. Young. The board seemed interested and ordered the department to investigate.

"It doesn't have to be done," says Frances, "as government is set up to do it." In the petition she cited reasons for a botanic garden such as its use as a local proving ground for plants, scientific research uses, and its utilization as "passive recreation." The county administration said, "no money," so Frances went to work organizing the "Foundation"—a non-profit group whose sole purpose was (and is) to provide funds and volunteer labor to get (and keep) the garden off the ground.

Plants were donated and set in during the two years that the county took to give final approval. Three years after Mrs. Young started the local botanic garden idea, forty thousand plants were donated and set in place. "We started the Foundation on $10 and $17,300 was in the fund nine years later.

"All kinds of excuses were given why it couldn't be done," says Frances. "If I'd followed procedure, none of it would be done now," she adds. "It amazes me when they tell you 'no' and just expect you to accept it." All but one of the buildings on the grounds were built by volunteer labor with donated materials from Los Angeles businesses. Frances was told that the manufacturers wouldn't donate all the materials she required, but nonetheless she tried, and they did donate (and often delivered those gifts from well over fifty miles away.)

For two years, all calls about the South Coast Botanic Garden came into Frances' patio-turned-workroom. That was "seven days a week, twenty-four hours a day," says Frances, "I look at it as being very serious but . . . I've had a lot of fun." Volunteers were the force supporting Mrs. Young. In one three-week period, thirty thousand plants were collected through donations. "I was the one with the big mouth," but, "I couldn't have done it without the volunteers," Frances emphasizes.

The volunteers worked around the landfilling operation which ended just over ten years ago. "Once they brought in two truckloads of *Life* magazines, and we couldn't get anything to grow over them." Frances told the Foundation that there was "too much life in the magazines, it didn't give the plants a chance." Actually the acidy ink used on the glossy paper was to blame. One other truckload intrigued the volunteer workers, "a load of cracked toilets was brought in, along with old lamp posts," and the workers immediately began picturing toilets overflowing with flowers surrounded by the old-fashioned lamp posts. Those materials, though, ended up under the botanic garden along with the rest of the problem-causing trash.

At the time of her pushing to get the garden approved, Frances was invited to join a senior citizens' group, but even though past sixty she "hadn't reached the age yet," Mrs. Young quipped. Now, "almost eighty," she still isn't old "enough to be a senior citizen."

The only problem Frances Young encountered working out the various methods of organizing the garden was, "frustration with government," but she found that it all depends on, "how you treat people, and how you accept those frustrations." Each volunteer workday that was held by the Foundation drew twenty to fifty workers. A small core of twenty showed up every weekend, to plant the areas that had been shaped by the large equipment after being filled. Frances also advises, "it's important getting people you can *work* with in government."

"It was a full-time job, and I made many new friends, and . . . I spent lots of money," states Mrs. Young. But, "to get it done there was no other way to do it. I'm a rebel," she understates. Once again she was told her plans would never come about.

But, ignoring the doom-sayers, the dedication consisted of a blessing by a Catholic priest, a Jewish rabbi, and a Protestant minister, "not each in a separate prayer," says Frances, "but one prayer together, from start to finish. To me that's the reason for

2-20: A couple walking upstream approaching the lake.
(Courtesy of Mark Wall)

2-21: The dedication by a rabbi, priest, and minister.
(Courtesy of Mark Wall)

the garden's success . . . our plants and flowers are gifts from our Creator. You may say God, Buddha, whatever—it matters not—it was given us by the Great Spirit."

That was sixteen years ago and over those years the lush escape from the nearby city clutter has amassed 200,000 plants, over 30 ducks, 150 carp, 2,000 goldfish, and numerous frogs, turtles, and crawfish. "It came out exactly as I had it pictured," confidently states Mrs. Young. Now the Foundation is an aide to the county, which supervises the garden. Edward Hartnagel, assistant superintendent of the grounds, describes a botanic garden as a "museum of plants." "We love it," said one elderly couple, "it's great to have someplace to walk."

The first thing that greets each of the 110,000 annual visitors is the wood-chip parking areas. "They are surprisingly trouble-free," according to Mr. Hartnagel. The only maintenance necessary is a weekly sweeping to move the misplaced chips back onto the parking areas.

Once out of their cars or buses the main attraction for visitors, especially the more than six thousand schoolchildren taken through each year, is the 1¾-acre lake leading into a 1,000-foot stream. "I come here to meditate; I'm not sure everybody likes that kind of stuff, but those that do *really* appreciate this place," stated one visitor.

Turning the barren landscape of the landfill into the lush, life-encouraging greenness of the garden was quite a benefit to local wildlife. Besides the wild birds, various other forms of wild-life proliferate—such as skunks and rabbits. Corn supplied by the Foundation for the ducks, and bread brought by visitors, works its way down the food chain through fish, crawfish, frogs, and turtles.

Occasionally, when the duck population gets too large, some are culled and taken to a nearby marsh and larger lake (also county-owned). At first rabbits and skunks presented seedlings and older plants problems by nibbling on them in force. They were trapped and released elsewhere, but, according to Mr. Hartnagel, there always seemed to be more and more of them. "Now we don't try to overcome it, we just try to live with it," adds Mr. Hartnagel. Since adopting this philosophy, the rabbit population has "stabilized itself," he concludes.

2-22: Hungry waddlers entertain a school tour.
(Courtesy of Mark Wall)

Six dozen volunteers yearly donate time as clerks, guides, craft makers, information window workers, and plant propagation helpers. In the school tours alone, volunteers have donated six thousand hours yearly. Many of these volunteers come from the more than five hundred members of the Foundation which just recently pledged $200,000 to build the new Frances Young meeting hall, and nearby offices. "They've done a lot," says Mr. Armand Sarinana, superintendent of the gardens.

Container gardening, bonsai culture, pond culture, plant identification, youth vegetable plots, and poisonous, medicinal, and edible plants are topics of some educational classes offered at the gardens. Another annual demonstration—pruning—was held for the first time not long ago. Two instructors were on hand for the thirty-five or so expected gardeners . . . four hundred people showed up for the class. Since then the class has expanded. The last pruning demonstration had eight instructors and a thousand participants. "It's nice to see my tax dollars going toward something peaceful," stated a visitor.

Frances Young recalls one youthful inner-city visitor on a

2-23: A high school volunteer waters the vegetable gardens.
(Courtesy of Mark Wall)

tour with his classmates through the gardens. The boy noticed a lizard and having never seen one, asked what it was, what it ate, everything about it. "He must have studied that lizard for forty-five minutes," says Frances. From then on he pleaded with Mrs. Young to let him take it home to show to his brother. Frances said no, that the lizard must remain for other observers, but he "so wanted to take that animal home to show to his brother."

"Exposing them to nature, and making them aware of it," is one of the things Eric Brooks likes best about his job (that of guiding the daily bus tours). "It's an attractive place to work, and very satisfying showing it to the public," adds Eric, "it's almost like therapy."

The people who daily enjoy this therapy, knowingly or un-knowingly, have a rebellious, "big-mouthed," never-accept-no, "not-quite-senior" citizen named Frances Young to thank for it.

But recycling areas for play and recreation purposes can be less demanding (but no less rewarding) than the experience of Mrs. Young. Take the case of the Sweeney family of Southern California, who spearheaded the effort to turn a sand hill into a well-landscaped hill entirely with volunteer labor and donated funds.

"It looked so futile, planting a little bush on such a massive hill of sand," Gail Sweeney says. "I planted a tree there when I was this tall," she adds, holding her hand at the level of her knee.

Indeed it must have looked futile to Gail who, at age ten, helped other volunteers turn a steeply angled pure sand hill into a landscaped and scenic park. Gail's father, Mike Sweeney, accepted the chairmanship of the Sand Dune Park Citizens' Committee soon after building plans were under way.

The sand pile rests on city property between an armory and an elementary school in Manhattan Beach. The city, in Los Angeles County, was selling the sand to local contractors—a fact which alone encouraged the insecure residents above the hill to push for park plans rather than risk sliding houses. A near-tragedy speeded up efforts to find another use for the lot when two cave-digging youths were nearly buried in a tunnel they had dug into the side of the hill. "Once it was developed we knew it would be safe for the kids," committee member Joan Dontan-ville says.

2-24: Gail Sweeney, volunteer.
(Courtesy of Mark Wall)

The residents went to the city council for funds to build the park. Unfortunately, the city couldn't spare the money, so the residents took it upon themselves. Professional plumbers, carpenters, engineers, the owner of a local trucking firm and many others donated their time, skills, and materials in creating the park. Many of these people were committee members and lived near the top of the sand hill. "Seventy-five percent of our labor was volunteer labor," according to Mike Sweeney. One woman donated 545 hours of her time in one year.

Although eleven hundred people were contacted by school hand-outs, weekend workdays brought out only twenty to thirty people to back up the group of eleven "undiscourageable" volunteers.

"We really needed citizen input," Mrs. Dontanville says, "and people really looked forward to working." Approximately one weekend a month was set aside as a working weekend. Small groups of volunteers planted, weeded, built, and just generally sweated. About 6,500 people-hours went into the park. "Most of the work was done by women's mouths," Mrs. Dontanville comments. "We conned people into picking up shovels."

Youth groups were "given" areas to plant and nurture. Women volunteers (including committee members) scrounged up cuttings and small plants—adding many living Christmas trees—according to Mike, and kept them in crowded backyards until planting could begin. In fact, scrounging was a regular part of the committee administration. Along with the Walkway, Playground, and Lighting divisions, an actual Scrounging division was formed and its project head chosen.

Almost three thousand railroad ties were donated by the local railroads, and excluding a few days' worth of digging by volunteers, the ties were free. The National Guard gave their time to saw and lay the ties in the walkways that climb the sand dune. The ties serve as retaining walls and steps. The National Guard also ran heavy equipment for playground facility placement and rough leveling.

Nearby cities have tried similar projects, but few were able to keep the organization and funds necessary for long-term work. But by Sand Dune Park's example (and those of Gail, Mike and Joan), it is possible to enlist community aid in building a lovely, landscaped park. Gail Sweeney, now twenty-six, concludes, "It's so pretty with the winding trails and all."

2-25: Sand Dune Park.
Swing set in use.
(Courtesy of Mark Wall)

2-26: Looking down the hill, over railroad tie path; foliage and playground at bottom.
(Courtesy of Mark Wall)

2-27: Close-up of path which makes use of donated railroad ties.
(Courtesy of Mark Wall)

2-28: Playground equipment and hill covered with donated plants.
(Courtesy of Mark Wall)

2-29: Retaining wall built with railroad ties and telephone poles.
(Courtesy of Mark Wall)

The various examples in this chapter suggest that "recycling for play" is not something that need be left to the local government. Individuals, such as Mrs. Frances Young, the Sweeneys and their volunteers, and others, forcefully demonstrate through their actions that it is indeed possible for an individual to bring about positive changes in the community. With these examples all of us can find some corner of our environment to make "playful," to turn green.

chapter 3

The Trail

by James C. McCullagh

If there is one thing true about America, it is that the country loves recreation and play. It loves long weekends, challenging sports, and innovative games.

This is the age of the outdoors. The age of the backpacker, the mountain climber, the rapids-runner. Of the hang glider. Of free-falling in space. Of hot-air balloons.

Backpackers will religiously travel miles, many miles, to get to the Appalachian Trail, to get to the Smokies, the Rockies, and the Ozarks.

A typical weekend scenario might begin something like this. A score of men and women leave work early on a Friday afternoon, jump in their cars, and, with plenty of beer and sandwiches, make a mad dash for the Cheat River in West Virginia where they hope that the rapids are swift and that the rocks are not out of the water.

During the half-day drive they talk about a lot of things, especially about the dull weekend they could be experiencing in New York, watching the Mets at Shea Stadium, or a bike race in Central Park.

No, they want none of that. They want the outdoors, the challenge of the water, the scent of danger, the thrill of the rocks. They want to be on the slippery side of death.

And they will pay any price to get there. They will travel hundreds, perhaps thousands of miles to get to a fresh, swift-water experience so that afterwards they can wear a T-shirt which boldly proclaims: "I Cheated the Cheat."

These are the people who know about the mundane world of modern sports. About the lack of competition in competitive sports. About the vulgar sport of auto racing—fumes, the roar, the wreck.

Yes, they moan about energy consumption in "dirty" sports but they don't think twice about expending gallons of fuel to get to that quiet spot where they can commune with nature.

One of the major ironies of the rush to the outdoors, the flight to clean recreation, is that few people realize the amount of energy—and we're consuming annually about five billion gallons of gasoline for recreation—that is required to transport them to their fresh-air sanctuaries.

The fact is that we can't sail like a bird on Saturday and Sunday but burn like a jet the rest of the week. We have to do better than that. Some have suggested that we take buses to the wilderness. Or triple up in cars, or take trains, or bikes, or walk. But we must do something.

Similarly, we should look at the quality of recreation that is built on the assumption of that "mad rush to the wilderness" where we can forget, at least for a few hours, the press of taxes.

Recreation and the Community

Instead of looking for more efficient ways to get to distant recreation sites, it might be more meaningful to consider, in this age of limits, alternative forms of recreation.

The editors of *RAIN* magazine have been eloquent in their plea for people to make the most of their community, to travel and play in their own backyards. "People travel for many reasons, yet very few of those reasons can best be satisfied by travel. Entertainment, rest, and 'getting away' can all take place in our own communities. Wise travel requires that we first minimize unnecessary travel by improving the places where we live and our relationship with the people with whom we live. We must then develop patterns of transportation, accommodation and recreation that require less energy and money to operate, create more direct and personal contact among people, and cause less damaging impact on the environment."

With seriousness and hyperbole the *RAIN* editors enjoin us, in the same poster, to "Stop Tourism—Make Where You Are

Paradise." Clearly the point of this is to encourage us all to look for recreation alternatives in our own backyards, in the spaces and the hearts of the community.

In a sense, Americans will have to learn how to play all over again. Perhaps this change of heart should start in the family. It might mean turning off the television and allowing family members to create, to throw shadows against the wall with their fingers, to get down on their hands and knees and play. Such simple forms of play, as you will see in later chapters, have not been forgotten.

But, as we have learned in previous chapters, enlightened recreation implies participation on some level in the construction of parks, playgrounds, and green spaces. But the list could also include anything that grows out of a community's wisdom and needs, including walking trails.

Of course, this is not easy or instant recreation, as Tom Yoannou of New York will attest. Yoannou, Director of Conservation and the Outdoors, is an avowed conservationist who freely admits that he discovered at age forty that "I was ignorant of our wider home, the earth. I didn't know anything about the soil, the natural processes, the laws of recycling. I didn't feel any responsibility for the earth. I would get my recreation and pleasure—my play—like anyone else and not think of where they came from. I knew nothing about biology. I did not know that trees have as much expanse below as above.

"Look at the tulip trees; they are snobs of the forest. Look at the natural stairs that nature provides to prevent runoff. Could any of us have invented that? Would you believe all of this is on Staten Island in New York City?" Most people would not. They don't believe that there is a real possibility of finding peace— that quiet place—and serenity within the city. You don't have to go on long vacations to the woods. You can find a trail or build a trail close to home. Something you can get to often. Something that will help you re-create yourself.

Yoannou is adamant about the need for recreation alternatives. "The ever-spreading urban sprawl," he writes, "eats up thousands upon thousands of acres of wooded and open land each year—farms, forests, and wetlands, and constantly shrinks the countryside. What is more, the distance between the inner cities and the open countries is increasing each year to the extent that it is already uneconomical to travel three, four, or five hours

3-1: Tom Yoannou—trailblazer.

to and from a given place to enjoy a day's outing. Obviously, there is no time left for enjoyment."

From the very beginning Yoannou's trail-building encountered difficulty, as his proposed route conflicted with plans for a new highway—the Richmond Parkway on Staten Island. But for well over a decade Yoannou and his volunteers persisted until they won the right to build a thirteen-mile trail through the island's Greenbelt.

The Staten Island Greenbelt Trail

Blazed blue and called the Greenbelt Circular, the trail rivals in beauty, maintenance and variations of terrain and setting the best trails in the New York metropolitan area. It is a multipurpose trail because most of it can be used not only for hiking, but for snowshoeing and horseback-riding as well. Then as a means of touring the Greenbelt it is unequaled because it takes the hiker through every place of importance: The glacial valley of the Clove Lakes Park, the many glacial ponds dotting the Richmond Escarpment, the Todt Hill (highest elevation along the eastern seaboard south of Maine), the Moravian Cemetery (burial place of Commodore Vanderbilt and his descendants), the High Rock Park Conservation Center, the restoration project of Colonial Richmondtown, the hills overlooking the Richmond Fresh Hills (the only river that starts and ends within city limits), etc. It is an educational trail as well, for in the process it touches on everything of botanical, geological and historical value in the Greenbelt. Opossums, muskrats and other small mammals live there, and few people know that the Greenbelt is still the home of the Great Blue Heron and that many bird species, above all the pheasant, abound there. Buck's Hollow in its northwest corner has been acclaimed by naturalists of the National Park Service as a model mini-wilderness in an urban setting. The trail, which is in an area easily accessible to the city dweller, constitutes the best form of both recreation and conservation.

Yoannou, who believes it is hedonism to think of recreation without conservation, has made his recreation a strong political statement and, with his volunteers, has saved a precious greenbelt.

While not all of us can stop highways or build trails of such magnitude, there are plenty of ways to discover trails close to home, as Tom Floyd, Supervisor of Trails, Potomac Appalachian Trail Club, suggests throughout the remainder of the chapter.

Discovering Trails Close to Home

I like to sit down with a map and trace out a good route for a new trail. It may be a trail across an extensive government forest or through a private farm, or ten or twenty private farms. The trail may cross entire mountain ranges, or lie within a small pastoral valley. It may be a long-distance route for backpack excursions or a short footpath for strolling.

Six months later, or a year or two years later, I like to go out to the area that I sketched on the map and walk the completed trail. While in the beginning it was just an idea, it is now a real pathway, cleared, graded, and marked. People are hiking it.

Sound like an airy dream? It needn't be if the idea is practical and there are people available who can organize to get a job done.

Garden for the Blind

3-2

3-3

3-4

3-2 through 3-5: Scenes from the Staten Island Greenbelt.

3-5

One thing is unquestionable. People need foot trails. They need places to walk, places far away and places close to home.

The members of the Potomac Appalachian Trail Club of Washington, D.C., spend a lot of their time tracing imaginary trails on maps. And they move right ahead searching out the land records, writing letters, visiting landowners, and building new trails. In the past four years, we have started with a few ideas and have gone on to build more than a hundred miles of new trails in the city, the suburbs, the rural areas, and the distant mountains. We hope to double or triple that number on other projects that we have already started.

Let's look at a few examples of our work. Bill and Kim Hutchinson of our club have spent many days scouting the Sugarloaf Mountain area of suburban Maryland, studying routes for a new trail network on two thousand acres of government land and several private parcels. To get this started, we simply wrote letters and paid visits to the state forest manager and one of the large landowners. The forester and the landowner liked the concept and asked us to begin the scouting. Later, they will review our specific route proposals. Then our volunteer members will blaze the new trails, and we'll appoint permanent overseers to do the upkeep.

On another new project, Dr. Clif Firestone, Bob Mroczek, and Jim Denham have been busy on several weekends reconnoitering ridgetops and rocky ravines in the Shenandoah Mountains in search of a good corridor for a new long-distance trail which will connect three existing trail systems. Most of the trail will be in George Washington National Forest. After conceiving the idea for this trail, we briefly discussed the proposal and marked maps showing the preferred general corridor. Forest supervisor George Smith soon expressed personal interest in the project and asked for more specific proposals, which Firestone's crew is preparing. Since the two-hundred-mile project extends beyond our usual range, we asked the Old Dominion Appalachian Trail Club of Richmond, Virginia, to take the lower half, and they quickly agreed. Their scouts are working from the south and will meet Firestone's group coming down from the north.

Near downtown Washington, we have started an extensive trail project in the two-thousand-acre Rock Creek Park, a national park woodland preserve in the heart of the District of Columbia. In this case, Jeff Norman, a volunteer friend of the park, contacted the club to ask if we would take on a project to build new trails in the city. Park manager Jim Redmond liked the idea and laid out several routes, mostly along footpaths grown over and abandoned from an era of fifty or sixty years ago when horse and foot travel were common.

For another project in the suburbs, club member Ken Jeffries came up with the idea of a new twenty-mile trail crossing two state parks, a city watershed, a small national park, and a few private parcels in the Catoctin Mountains of Maryland. Most of the landowners and agencies have already approved the route, and our volunteer work crews have cleared the first four miles.

Our biggest recent success story has been the Big Blue Trail, a 140-mile foot trail that will go across 70 miles of private land. Let's take a close look at this one, and see how ordinary people can get a trail started.

Fred Blackburn of our club, assisted by Jim Denton and Woody Kennedy, laid out the first half of the trail, mostly in

3-6: Landscape architect Shirley Street and volunteer supervisor of trails, Tom Floyd, planning new trails for the National Children's Island in Washington, D. C.
(Courtesy of Michael F. Parks)

3-7: Volunteer trail-builders constructing a new footpath in
the Lena Artz Woods near Washington, D.C.
(Courtesy of Hugh Stokely)

Shenandoah National Park and George Washington National Forest. I took over at Blackburn's request to build the last seventy miles of the trail ending at the Potomac River.

Since no arrangements had been made with the landowners, I had to start from scratch. First, I purchased about fifteen U.S. Geological Survey maps and pasted them together to form one large map of the area. These maps show all features of the land including terrain, contours, elevation, and the locations of buildings, roads, old trails, streams, and power lines. The color maps also show the forests and open fields. The maps may be obtained by writing the U.S. Geological Survey, Washington, D.C.

After I pieced the maps together, I traced out possible routes for the trail. Then, during the next few weeks, I drove to the area several times to get the "feel" of the land. I made a few changes in my tentative route and finally came up with a general corridor that passed through fifty miles of private land and twenty miles of state hunting preserves. The private land was divided about equally between valley farms and mountain forests. The state land was under control of the game and fish commission.

The next step was to find out who owned the private land. This took about a week of my vacation time as I visited county courthouses and searched land records. At each courthouse, I went first to the county clerk's office to examine tax maps, deeds, and survey plates. It was not too difficult to transfer the land boundaries to the USGS maps.

From the county treasurer's office, I obtained the mailing addresses of about two hundred landowners on or near the tentative route.

Up to this point, I had not talked to many landowners. Those whom I did visit reacted suspiciously, as one might expect if a stranger walks in cold and asks for permission to place a public footpath across their private land. After about five consecutive rejections, I stopped this approach.

I then wrote letters individually tailored to each landowner, explaining the project, the purpose of the trail, and a brief history of our club and its record with other landowners. I enclosed a printed flyer about the trail. In each letter, I asked for permission to route the trail across the landowner's property, indicating the preferred route—usually close to boundary lines or in the woods—and told him that if I didn't receive a reply I would come visiting.

Only about 15 percent of the people responded, but most of these gave permission. I revised the proposed route to try to link up the land parcels where permission had been given. Then I wrote more letters, mentioning the names of other people in the area who had given permission.

When I made the follow-up visits, most of the people responded very favorably. Some of them introduced me to their neighbors—and all of them gave permission. They didn't know me, but they knew their neighbors, and that made all the difference.

In the end, I sent out about 150 letters and made about sixty personal follow-up visits or, in a few cases, phone calls. I did not contact the other eighty landowners whom I had written, since my final trail route would not need to cross their land.

In all, more than 80 percent of the people that I visited gave permission. As an aside, I will mention that a friend who was working on another trail project gave up when he received only one reply after writing ten letters. Convinced that the project was a loser, he didn't make even one follow-up visit.

This experience convinces me that a combination of letters, printed material, and follow-up visits, combined with an ability to meet and deal with people—to talk land in their terms—is the key to a successful trail project.

About half of the landowners along the Big Blue Trail live on their land, and the others are absentee landowners, mostly business and professional people from the cities who use the land for vacation property. I found that the two groups, the farmers and the city people, were equally cooperative in granting permission to use their land for the trail. Both groups were quite sophisticated in expressing concern about land-use and the quality of the environment.

Two of the landowners liked the trail so much that they joined the club, and four others volunteered to let us use their land for backpacker campgrounds.

Two of the owners donated land to the club, a total of 65 acres. Part of this was an easement, where the trail right-of-way is permanently protected and the landowners and their heirs relinquish the right to cut timber or construct buildings. The club later purchased an additional 55 acres, making a total of 120 acres protecting six miles of the trailway. A few owners signed cooperative land-use agreements, and the others gave

3-8: Volunteer trail-builders constructing a trail in a wooded
area near Washington, D.C.
(Courtesy of Hugh Stokely)

written or oral permission. The state game and fish commission gave written consent.

The actual clearing, construction, and marking of the trail is being done by our club's volunteers. We announce the work trips in the club's monthly publication and the local newspapers, and the people show up in good numbers. They come from all backgrounds. On one recent weekend, we had two physicists, a sheet metal mechanic, a college professor, a civil engineer, a taxi driver, four secretaries, a librarian, three retired people, and several high school and college students. They ranged in age from thirteen to sixty-three.

On the work trips, an experienced club member will range ahead of the others to flag the route for the trail. Ideally, the trail will go through a variety of terrain and habitat, weaving through rock formations, striking out across valleys and hollows, bending gradually and expectantly, and cutting sharply up graded switchbacks to a mountaintop and the gradual unfolding of a magnificent view.

While most of the trail will require cutting small trees and brush (often along abandoned trails and old logging roads), some of the route along the cross-section of a steep hillside will also need to be dug out and formed into a trail shoulder, where the trail edge will be shored up with rocks and logs. A few trenches will have to be dug to divert water off the trail. But for the most part, this heavier work isn't needed.

The completed trail should be a work of art—a pathway that will lead the hiker expectantly through the forest, blending harmoniously with trees, laurel, rocks, and moss. It should be a window to the outdoors. A good trail will stimulate thought and discussion.

I usually don't spend a lot of time hiking the new trails. I'm too busy drawing new lines on maps, bushwhacking through the woods, and building other new pathways. Trailblazing itself is my recreation.

Anyone who wants to experience the excitement of trail-building should contact an organized hiking or trail club like PATC, or form a new one. An existing service-type club might be able to do the job.

A few people have done it alone, or nearly so. Grandma Gatewood, the Appalachian Trail hiker, blazed a fifteen-mile trail across her county in Ohio, doing all the landowner contacts and other work by herself. She was in her seventies. Randy Saliga of Alexandria, Virginia, maintains a trail on his own for the National Park Service. He was sixteen when he took on the project.

Sandy and Kathy MacNabb are typical of about two hundred people who oversee and maintain PATC's finished trails. They cleared a three-mile stretch of the Big Blue Trail and are now maintaining it—and asking for more.

Club member Sam Samuelson, seventy-two, an almost legendary trailblazer in Virginia, has for years maintained a fifteen-mile trail in a remote mountain area of George Washington National Forest. Often, he packs in for several days, camping alone in deep wilderness, clearing the trails of fallen trees and limbs, cutting back new growth, and checking erosion.

Pioneer Herman Nolte has maintained a section of the club's Appalachian Trail for over forty-five years. Hiker Frank Shelburne has led several expeditions for the club scouting new trail corridors in the rugged Blue Ridge Mountains. In the inner city, Frank Collins is working on new trails for children at an unlikely site, an island in Washington, D.C.'s Anacostia River. In the Pond Mountains outside the suburbs, Neale Schumann is building a new trail for blind students and another for scientific education.

Trailblazer Jeannette Fitzwilliams opened and now maintains twenty-five miles of foot trails for backpackers in the distant Monongahela National Forest. Author-hiker Ed Garvey and Ray Fadner have opened new trails for PATC. The late Myron Avery and Frank Schairer built several hundred miles of the famous Appalachian Trail.

Altogether, the trail crews of the Potomac Appalachian Trail Club devote over ten thousand hours of their time every year to trail building and maintenance. Presently, they are mother hen to 600 miles of foot trails, and they're shooting for 250 more. It may be work, but they call it fun.

See the Appendix for a partial list of trail organizations which you can contact if you are interested in constructing trails close to home.

by Waldo J. Nielsen

chapter 4
The Space

When you think about trails the image that probably comes to mind is one of a narrow, foot-beaten path traversing a wooded area and either going uphill or downhill. As a matter of fact, the dictionary defines a trail as a path or track made by man or animal across a "wild region" or over "rough country." This image is accompanied by another image, and that is one of a person with a heavy knapsack and well-shod in hiking boots.

Most of the established trails in the United States, and for that matter, in many other countries, are trails of this type, generally located in high or hilly country and, for the most part, following the ridges and crests of the mountains or hills. And they are rightly called hiking or backpacking trails. This is understandable since these trails were promoted and laid out by hiking and mountaineering groups and organizations. Also, much of the land available for lengthy trails was found only in the mountains or hilly areas.

Trails

All well and good. These established trails serve a great need and have afforded pleasure to thousands of people for years. As a matter of fact, there is a need for more trails of this type since many of the established trails are suffering from overuse. However, these trails serve a somewhat limited population: those who have the time and wherewithal to travel long distances to reach them. This potential population is also limited to those who have the necessary physical stamina and excludes very young children, the handicapped, many older people and persons not in the best of health, as well as those who desire more convenient recreation outlets. These trails do not overly encourage family hiking, especially if grandma and grandpa are along. And this need can be satisfied by a conscious effort to explore recreation alternatives within and close to the community.

Now let us expand upon the definition of a trail. Let us think in terms of a lane, a pathway, a corridor, a right-of-way, a canyon or a river, and their potential for use as recreation-ways. Another way of looking at this is to think in terms of linear space.

Linear Space

What is linear space? Linear space is a relatively narrow strip of land extending for some distance. It can be either man-made or natural. Man-made spaces are strips of land based on some facility, either past or existing, which required or requires such strips of land for transportation, communication or distribution. These are the abandoned railroad rights-of-way, transmission lines, canal towpaths, aqueduct or sewer easements, pipelines, levees, survey lines, abandoned wagon roads, greenbelts, etc. Natural spaces can be river banks, dry creeks, arroyos and canyons.

Let us explore this a little further. Because this is essentially what we will be doing—exploring, discovering and creating our own linear space, or, to be more exact, recreation-ways.

Land or open space for recreation is becoming increasingly scarce and very expensive. We have, for too long, thought in terms of large chunks of land for recreation and play, whether it be a state park or a playground. But if we think in terms of linear space, we are thinking about land which may already be available for recreational use, since the trail or pathway does not have to be cut through or blazed—it is already there. This availability, together with the minimal need for development, should result in lower overall costs. As railroad abandonment increases, more of these strips should become available. Also, as more sewer interceptors and pipelines are built, the opportunity to obtain easement on the rights-of-way is increasing.

In his book, *The Last Landscape*, William H. Whyte points

out that long, narrow strips of land are one of the most efficient forms of open space per acre. It is a perimeter or edge of an open space that provides the maximum physical access and the maximum visual impact. For instance, one square mile of land in the shape of a square has four miles of perimeter. One square mile of land in the form of a strip sixty-six feet wide would be virtually all ·perimeter, 160 miles. Many railroads and canals were built one chain (sixty-six feet) wide, as were many of our older roads. Another way of putting it is that one mile of railroad right-of-way contains eight acres. How much useful, conventional parkland would that give us?

Perhaps one of the outstanding features of linear space, whether man-made or natural, is the fact that segments of linear space are widely distributed throughout most states. And, perhaps even more important, many of them are located in and near urban areas where there is a great need for trails. The New York State Barge Canal, which is in the process of becoming a cross-state recreational facility, with a continuous hiking and bicycling path as well as a continuous waterway, passes through twenty-one counties with a combined population of over four million people, two-thirds of which is in urbanized areas.

Many of these segments of linear space lend themselves to multiple use. Most of these corridors or pathways are fairly level. Certainly they can all be walked. And if the path is smooth, such as a cindered railroad bed, it would be ideal for jogging. Also, if continuous for some distance, and not interrupted by unbridged streams, it might be feasible for bicycling. In the winter these pathways might be ideal for cross-country skiing. All of these activities can be combined with nature study and birdwatching. Additionally, they are ideal for family walking, for the older hiker and perhaps for the hiker not in the best of health.

Abandoned railroad rights-of-way, abandoned canal towpaths, and even abandoned roads, are natural resources, just as are our streams, forests, marshes and mountains. Putting them to use as recreation-ways would be recycling at its best. The utilization of existing transmission lines, pipelines and sewer easements as recreation-ways would be multiple use at its best. There is probably no better way to recycle for play.

Now we come to a feature of these rights-of-way that is somewhat unique. The abandoned railroad rights-of-way and canal towpaths span not only space but also time. The building of the canals and railroads, and their ever westward movement, is a great part of the history of the United States. Walking these rights-of-way is like walking through history. As one rambles along, one sees the abandoned stations, the abandoned farms and the ghost towns. Perhaps the railroad may follow an old canal towpath; the remains of old locks may be there to discover. On some rights-of-way the tunnels are still there to walk through and the switchbacks to climb. This all adds up to another bonus: in addition to the healthy exercise and mental relaxation of walking, they add another dimension—the fun of exploring.

On the Trail

Now that I have described some of the features and advantages of these different types of linear space, it might be worthwhile to narrate some personal experiences on these trails of discovery.

The Fifty-Mile Hike

A number of years ago, my hiking companion, Ralph Colt of Rochester, New York, and I were planning to hike fifty miles in one day. This was the time when the fifty-miler was receiving much publicity due to President Kennedy's deep interest in physical fitness. Now where can one hike fifty miles in one day? It would be very difficult if not impossible to do this on one of New York's many fine hiking trails, which, for the most part, are located in hilly or mountainous country. Walking along a road would be unpleasant and unsafe. And it would be ridiculous to walk around and around in a circle for fifty miles.

It occurred to Ralph and myself that there are ideal trails for an adventure of this sort. Long stretches of level and clear path—abandoned railroad rights-of-way. We chose an abandoned roadbed which is ideal for trails: the New York Ontario and Western Railway, which, in effect, is a linear path running 260 miles through New York State from Fulton (near Oswego) to Cornwall-on-the-Hudson. It runs through some of the most scenic countryside in the state without hitting any of the large towns or cities (probably one of the reasons for its demise).

4-1: The cindered path of a roadbed is ideal for jogging, particularly if it's close to the community.

We started out at 5:00 a.m. on a cold and windy day in April. For the most part the roadbed had a pleasant walking surface of cinders. As a rule, when tracks and ties are removed, the roadbed is smoothed out and a flat, level surface of cinders, earth, or rock ballast is left. Many of the bridges had been removed when the ties and tracks were taken up. This necessitated some waist-high creek fording and some detours.

The roadbed traversed fields, swampland and woods. Usually the roadbed was built on fill, especially in the swampy areas where it was built up to heights of ten or fifteen feet. In other sections the roadbed was cut through small hillocks. It was interesting to see how the necessary drainage facilities were constructed. For the most part the roadbed was bordered by farmland and at one point we had to share it with some grazing cows. Then there was quite a change in the vista when it ran along the northern shore of Lake Oneida.

Twenty hours later, footsore and weary, we limped back to our starting point at Fulton. It was this hike which whetted our appetites and got us interested in the utilization of abandoned railroad rights-of-way for hiking trails, an interest which has not diminished.

There is an interesting footnote to this. At the time of our hike, this right-of-way, which had been taken over by the New York State Department of Public Works, had several "No Trespassing" signs. Ten years later, this entire section had been converted into a snowmobile trail by Oneida County and the New York State Department of Transportation. All the missing bridges had been replaced, and would you believe, they had actually constructed a covered bridge over a river. You might be interested to know that when I bicycled over this roadbed in the summer I did not run into any snowmobiles.

Ghost Trains in the Maine Woods

In my reading I had come across mention of the "Ghost Trains in the Maine Woods." Two large steam locomotives were in the middle of the Maine woods, one hundred miles from the nearest railhead and forty miles from the nearest town, left there when the railroad was abandoned forty years ago. They were part of a logging railroad which moved logs from Eagle

Lake to Chesuncook Lake, where they were then floated down the Penobscot River to the paper mills. They had been brought in over the ice by special Lombard log haulers years before and it would have been too expensive to haul them out for scrap.

At first, we had wanted to hike in on the ten miles of the Eagle Lake and West Branch roadbed to see these locomotives. Both the forest warden and the park ranger of the Allaghash Wilderness waterway very strongly suggested we not attempt this since the roadbed was almost completely overgrown with full-sized trees. We then decided to hike in on another linear right-of-way. This was a shorter route where a telephone line once ran into the Eagle Lake terminus of the logging railroad.

Even then people thought we were crazy to attempt this. After all, no one hikes into this region; everyone goes in by canoe, motorboat or even by plane. We started at the Chamberlain Lake lock dam where we met Mr. and Mrs. Milford Kidney, who tend the lock dam. Mrs. Kidney has written a book, *Away From It All*, about their first years in this wilderness, miles from their nearest neighbors.

4-2: An abandoned roadbed near Rochester, New York, where an entire family can walk together.

The trail was a downed telephone line. The trail markers were the porcelain insulators, some on the ground and some on the trees. This was literally a "trail of insulators." It is very easy to get lost in the Maine woods; this hike would have been very difficult to attempt without these wonderful trail markers.

It is an almost uncanny sight to emerge from a dark, narrow trail into the sunlight and find yourself looking at these two giant locomotives, left in solitary seclusion where they were abandoned over forty years ago. We stayed overnight, and when we returned the next day we were told by the Kidneys that we were the first people to backpack into that area since they first came to the lock dam—fifteen years before.

A Trek across Tug Hill

If you look at a map of New York State you will notice a large area untraversed by roads. This is the Tug Hill plateau, west of Boonville and south of Watertown. This has been referred to as one of the "empty areas" on the map. The environment is so hostile that no one, not even the Indians, ever attempted to settle on this plateau. Winters bring total snowfalls of well over three hundred inches, with depths up to twenty feet or more.

Perhaps it was this desolation which appealed to us. Wouldn't it be interesting to backpack across this plateau? However, there were no established hiking trails in this region. But there was, you guessed it, an abandoned railroad right-of-way. This was the old Glenfield and Western, a logging railroad which went twenty miles into the plateau from the town of Glenfield.

The roadbed, climbing the escarpment from the east, was almost completely overgrown. Nature reclaims its own quickly. This is the case with logging railroads where substantial roadbeds are not the rule. However, once on top we found that a good portion of the roadbed had been converted into a private dirt road. The Georgia Pacific lumber company, which owns virtually the entire plateau, leases land to hunting clubs on the plateau and this road provides access to the land.

We came across the ghost hamlets of Page and Monteola, once beehives of logging activity. Further on, the roadbed traversed beautiful wooded areas which offered respite on a hot sunny day. The right-of-way terminated near an old logging road which served as our exit from Tug Hill.

Where Is the Space?

It would be impossible to list and locate all of these pieces of linear space even if I just limited the list to man-made corridors or rights-of-way. Even if it were possible, this would be defeating the purpose of our book. A good deal of the fun of play comes in discovering these segments of linear space for ourselves. What can compare to your coming across an old weed-hidden canal lock enticing you to follow the old towpath? Or to finding an abandoned railroad roadbed and following its path through the meadows or woods? What about the right-of-way over an underground aqueduct or pipeline? What kind of trail will it make? There is only one way to find out—walk it.

In this section, I will discuss some of the characteristics of different types of linear space, give some examples of each type and mention where further information can be obtained.

Abandoned Railroad Rights-of-Way

Clearly I am referring to abandoned railroads where the ties and tracks have already been removed. Under no circumstances walk on or alongside existing tracks. There was a case a few years ago where three young people were killed by a train after making camp right on the tracks; they apparently thought the railroad had discontinued running.

Abandoned railroad rights-of-way are much more numerous both in mileage and in the number of such strips than any other type of right-of-way. Between 1937 and 1973, over 35,000 miles of railroad have been abandoned in the United States and with the recent railroad reorganization in the Northeast, additional thousands are slated to be abandoned. They are widely distributed throughout most states and form a network of potential trail systems in some states. These roadbeds are level (railroads rarely exceeded a 3 percent grade), well drained (for the most part), clear (the cinders are responsible for this), and self-contained (since the grade generally was built on fill or in a cut).

Roadbeds abandoned since 1960 are generally in the best condition for hiking and bicycling. They would be relatively free of undergrowth and are probably still fairly well drained. Many of the bridges have been left in place since the price for scrap iron was depressed in the sixties. These are the roadbeds which probably offer the best potential for recreational use.

Roadbeds abandoned between 1945 and 1960 vary considerably in their condition. Many sections have been completely obliterated by road construction or even farmed over. Most steel bridges were removed for their scrap value. Much of the roadbed is overgrown to some extent; this can range from knee-high brush to shoulder-high saplings. If these roadbeds have been used as farm roads or trails, they will probably still be in good condition. This undergrowth is not so much a problem in open semi-arid areas in the West.

Roadbeds abandoned prior to 1945 are in many cases almost completely obliterated and are quite difficult to locate even where they still exist. Some, however, depending upon soil conditions and climate, are surprisingly well preserved.

It should be pointed out that much of this abandoned roadbed has been sold to utility companies, landowners, farmers, fish and game clubs, etc. Some has been sold to salvage companies who in turn attempt to sell piecemeal what they can. Some has reverted to the original landowner if so stipulated in the deed and some is still owned by the railroad. Some is owned by the county or other local municipality. For the most part this land has not been posted.

Considering the thousands of abandoned railroad rights-of-way, surprisingly few have actually been converted into established trails which are marked and maintained. The outstanding example is the famous Wisconsin Bike Trail which runs thirty-two miles on the old Chicago and Northwestern roadbed between Sparta and Elroy. This roadbed had been surfaced with limestone screenings to provide a smoother surface for bicycles. The bridges were planked and picnic areas built. The trail goes through three 100-year-old tunnels which certainly adds variety to the hike or ride and should be refreshingly cool on a hot day.

Again, Wisconsin appears to be in the lead, with its twenty-three-mile Sugar River Trail between New Glarus and Brodhead, and a number of other trails on rights-of-way. New York State has plans for utilizing five different rights-of-way in the central part of the state, and some counties are utilizing shorter segments for bike trails. Not too long ago the Western Maryland Railroad donated about sixty miles of its right-of-way from the border near Frostburg, Maryland, to Connellsville, Pennsylvania, to the Western Pennsylvania Conservancy, which will in turn transfer it to

4-3

4-4

4-5

4-3 through 4-6: A recovered space: The C & O Canal.

4-6

the state of Pennsylvania. This promises to be an extremely scenic hiking trail as it winds its way along the Youghiogheny River.

As interesting as these established trails may be, I have found the non-designated rights-of-way more interesting, mainly because they are waiting there to be "discovered." There is a book which lists and maps the abandonments between 1937 and 1973 for each state, *Right-of-Way, A Guide to Abandoned Railroads in the United States.* This book is basically a guide to the general location of the abandoned railroads, listing the mileage abandoned and the end points of the abandoned segments, accompanied by a map of each state showing these abandonments.

A road map should suffice to get you to the vicinity of one of the end points. To locate the roadbed itself, you will have to make local inquiry or drive on roads crossing the right-of-way. Physical evidence of the abandoned roadbed is not hard to detect. The best maps to use are the topographic maps of the U.S. Geological Survey. The 7½-minute quadrangle maps quite often depict the abandoned grade; if not, it is readily discernible by the fills and cuts on the map. Most of the 15-minute quadrangle maps are being discontinued. You may be fortunate enough to locate some of the old 15-minute maps dating back to 1900 or 1905. These are a find since they show all the railroads. However, do not rely on them as a road map.

Early abandonments, especially those prior to 1945, will take some skill in locating. A knowledge of railroad construction comes in handy. In this case you should determine where the best location for a railroad would have been.

It should be pointed out that in addition to the above-listed rights-of-way there are thousands of abandoned interurban railroads, terminal and switching railroad lines. Many of these are in or very close to urban areas. Since many of them ran right through the cities and towns, and alongside highways which were later widened, it might be very difficult to trace some of them.

Now it is up to you to find your own right-of-way.

Canals

Before the railroads came the canals. In the latter part of the nineteenth century there were close to four thousand miles

4-7: Bicycling and hiking the Old Erie Canal State Park.

of canals in operation in this country. Even then there were some that had already been abandoned, a process which mushroomed as the railroads began taking over. In some cases the towpath was used for a railroad roadbed. An example is the ninety-mile Pennsylvania Railroad between Rochester and Olean, New York, built on the abandoned Genesee Valley Canal. The railroad has also been abandoned.

The towpaths were, of course, level, with grades being surmounted by locks. These can make ideal walking and jogging pathways as well as bicycle trails.

An outstanding example of a canal which has been converted into a recreation-way is the Chesapeake and Ohio Canal running from Georgetown in Washington, D.C., to Cumberland, Maryland, a distance of 184 miles. The towpath is ideal for walking, jogging and bicycling and it is gratifying to see how extensively it is used. Many of the old wood locks are still in place, and the lock-tenders' houses and some of the old taverns which hosted the travelers of long ago are still standing. Especially fascinating is the section of the canal as it winds its way alongside the river across from Harpers Ferry.

Another example is the Old Erie Canal State Park, a section of the old Erie Canal between Rome and DeWitt, near Syracuse, New York, which is still used as a feeder for the New York State Barge Canal. The towpath is being converted into a wide, smooth bicycle path with the old aqueducts now carrying bike traffic instead of barges.

Although we are talking mostly about abandoned canals, there are some operating canals that can serve as recreation-ways. An outstanding example is the 363-mile New York State Barge Canal between the Hudson River and Lake Erie which is being made into a cross-state recreation facility in addition to its use for commercial traffic and recreational boating. It will carry a cross-state hiking and bicycling pathway. The Barge Canal, completed in 1920, uses natural waterways and lakes and has no need for a towpath although the canalized sections have an adjoining service road which will be serving as the trail. Because

4-8

4-8 through 4-11: A discovered family recreation area: the Hugh Moore Canal, Easton, Pennsylvania.

4-9

4-10

4-11

of this, some detours will be necessary; perhaps an abandoned railroad right-of-way or two could be used. Someday you should be able to hike or bike across New York State on the level.

There are some maps which show all the early canals. Again, these would show only the general location. Now it is up to you to find the canal remains yourself.

Transmission Lines

Transmission or power lines literally criss-cross the country-side. If you were to stop your car at any point on a road, the chances are that you would be able to see a transmission line of some sort from where you stand.

When a line was built, the land directly under the line was probably cleared for access. There is no reason to keep it cleared, and, in time, there will probably be some fairly heavy growth. Nonetheless, the trace is still there and it can be used as a walking trail, perhaps to serve as a link between other rights-of-way. For the most part, these lands are privately owned with the utility company merely obtaining easement for its line; therefore, they may well be posted.

Still, there are a few cases where a utility owns the right-of-way and may have granted easement to a local community for use as a trail. The well-known Illinois Prairie Path, a thirty-mile hiking and bicycling trail west of Chicago, consists in part of an easement on a Commonwealth Edison Company trans-mission line right-of-way.

Aqueducts

Normally we think of aqueducts as stately pieces of stone-work supporting a trough through which water courses. Of course, it has been centuries since they were used to supply water to cities. Water is now supplied through underground conduits or tunnels, but they are still called aqueducts. For reasons of security and maintenance, the land above the tunnel is held as a right-of-way by the municipality. These rights-of-way are gen-erally kept in good shape.

One of these, the old Croton Aqueduct, running for thirty-two miles from the Croton Dam to the Harlem River in the Bronx, has been designated as a bicycling and hiking trail. Although a number of detours are necessary, this is an example of a much-needed pathway in a metropolitan area. More recently, 67 miles of the 444-mile California Aqueduct has been opened to bicycling. This is an open cut aqueduct and the bike path runs adjacent to the twenty-foot-wide service road along the aqueduct.

There may be an aqueduct near you. The appropriate USGS map will show it.

Levees

Levees are another possibility. Similar in some respects to an open cut aqueduct, the top of the embankment is generally wide enough to permit walking. Quite often when the Corps of Engineers channelized a river or stream, a levee-type embankment was constructed.

There has been a proposal to utilize the thirteen-hundred-mile Rio Grande levee between Brownsville and El Paso, Texas, as a recreational trail. The floodplain between the river and the levee is being used for camping.

In some respects, hiking or bicycling along a levee, an open cut aqueduct or an existing canal is similar to a walk along a river or lake. There is something refreshing about walking along a body of water—the view, a sense of coolness, whatever—it's a nice feeling.

Abandoned Roads

What with the proliferating highway construction, you might be surprised to know that roads have also been abandoned. As a matter of fact, before the turn of the century there were more roads than there are today. This was primarily because there were many more farms and most of these roads were farm roads. There were also many town and country roads that have since been abandoned. These were, for the most part, dirt and gravel roads which are slowly reverting to forest land. As a matter of

4-12: Making use of roadbed under expressway in Baton Rouge, Louisiana.

fact, in New England, where at one time about 80 percent of the land was open land (logged and farmed), approximately the same fraction has now reverted to woods.

My favorite abandoned roads are in the Adirondacks. These were not farm roads but wagon and stage roads. Built in the 1820s and 1830s and falling into disuse before the turn of the century, they are very difficult to locate. Unless continued in use as a logging road or trail, parts of these roads would now be almost completely obliterated. They were nothing more than ruts in the forest with sections of corduroy where needed. They are the old Albany Road which ran between Russel and Lake Pleasant, New York, the Canton to Chester Road and the Westport to Hopkinton Road. You won't find these on the road maps. As a matter of fact, considerable research is required, starting with nineteenth century maps which, at best, indicated an approximate route, which then should be traced on the appropriate U.S.G.S. topographic maps. Who knows, you might be able to find your own old wagon road.

Perhaps not as historically interesting, but closer to home, are some of the many abandoned town and country roads. Again, one has to work from old maps to locate them. True, some of these old roads may be impossible for bicycling or jogging, but the thrill in discovering them cannot be matched.

Underground Sewers and Pipelines

Similar to underground aqueducts, but much more numerous, are underground sewers, interceptors and pipelines. As more sewage treatment plants are built, connections have to be made. The land above the conduits or pipelines is part of the easement and buildings are generally prohibited on these rights-of-way.

Quite often these interceptors parallel rivers and streams. Ideally, a joint use easement should be obtained when they are being built. Such an undertaking has been successful in the town of Penfield, near Rochester, New York, where a trail is being built above a new interceptor line which follows the scenic Irondequoit Creek. As a matter of fact, this is referred to as a linear park because it actually connects or links a number of town parks along the creek.

4-13: Tolt Pipeline, Seattle, Washington.

Take a look at your own town or county park system. Are there any possibilities for linking them together? This could be a useful and interesting project and think of the thrill you would get if you were the one to discover the linkages.

This brings to mind what must be one of the outstanding linkages that ever took place. In the 1920s, Robert Moses was thinking about providing "parks for people" on Long Island and about building parkways so people could get to them. Looking at maps, he "discovered" that these linkages already existed in the form of underground aqueduct rights-of-way owned by the New York City Board of Water Supply. It was then a simple matter of transferring above-ground ownership to a different government agency.

Survey Lines

There may not be many of these around, but if you can find one, you've really found something. When a survey line was run, a trail was blazed. The most famous one, of course, is the Mason-Dixon Line which established the border between Maryland and Pennsylvania in 1784. Now part of this line is accessible because a utility company is cutting a thirty-five-foot swath for its gas line right-of-way on the exact path of the survey.

Some time ago, Boy Scouts from southwestern Pennsylvania found that some of the original markers were still standing. They were planning to blaze a trail along the line which, of course, had become heavily overgrown. And along came the utility company to blaze the trail for them. Working with the utility company, the Scouts have, to date, designated a twenty-nine-mile hiking trail.

This section can be reached by traveling one mile south out of Markleysburg, Pennsylvania, on an unmarked road which looks like it is in the last stages of abandonment. It can also be reached on Route 281 and Route 42 from Markleysburg, Route 381 from Elliotsville and Route 857 from Fairchance.

Most of the early land purchases had to be surveyed the hard way—on foot. Perhaps there are some survey lines in your state which might merit consideration for a trail. Just the fact that they are of historical interest might make it easier to generate local interest in such a project.

City Walks

Wherever there are sidewalks, there is a place to walk. Pounding pavement is all right but it can be made more interesting.

The Freedom Trail in Boston comes to mind. Many other cities have mapped walking tours. If your city or town doesn't have one, why not map one out? A tour of places of historic interest. Or a tour of interesting older homes and buildings—a sort of landmark tour. Or a tour along the waterfront. This can be limited only by your imagination. For example, a number of city tours are outlined in *The Gentle Art of Walking*, by George D. Trent, which is one of the most delightful books on walking that I have ever read.

River Walks

I have discussed potential pathways along canals, levees and open cut aqueducts, and mentioned the refreshing experience of walking along a body of water. Unfortunately, in this country, most lakefront, bayfront and riverfront property is privately owned and not open to the public. Unlike Europe and Canada, this country did not recognize this need until too late. In the past few years there has been increasing debate on this problem of public access to the waterfront. San Antonio, with its Paseo del Rio, or River Walk, is an outstanding example of what can be done.

If you look hard enough, you might be able to find some sections of riverfront that might be accessible. I am not referring to public parkland along a lakefront or riverfront—presumably you know about them already. I am referring to riverfronts which might have had mills and factories, now abandoned, along the banks. I am referring to rivers where the banks are too steep to have encouraged building of any sort. If a railroad runs along the river, the land between the tracks and the river is another possibility. Although the land might still be privately owned, it might not have seen use in years and might be virtually deserted. So it might be worth a ramble. And if promising enough, perhaps a campaign should be started to place it in public ownership.

Trails on the Rock

If you can walk along the river banks and on dry land, what about walking in the creek? On a dry river bottom. Or, if and when the water is low enough, going from rock to rock—call it rock scampering. It is guaranteed to make you feel like a ten-year-old, and it is surprising how far you can go in this manner.

Again, if the water is low enough, what about walking in the water itself? But bring along an extra pair of sneakers just for this purpose—the rocks can be mighty hard on bare feet. Recently we hiked along a three-mile section on the roadbed of the abandoned Pennsylvania Railroad between Tuscarora and Sonyea, New York. This roadbed was built on the towpath of the abandoned Genesee Valley Canal through the beautiful Keshaqua gorge. We returned by a different route: we walked down the middle of Keshaqua Creek. We scampered from rock to rock where possible or walked right through the water, which was rarely more than a foot deep. Needless to say, this can only be done at certain times of the year when the water is low enough. And on a hot summer day, believe me, it's really refreshing. Now there may be a dry river bottom or creek near you. Try it, you'll like it.

You might have read about rim-rock hopping or slickrocking. This is nothing more than canyon hiking—walking along the canyon bottom or working up and down the ledges. However, extreme caution is necessary. Flash floods are always a possibility. If the canyon is remote, or if it is more than a few hours' walk, it will be necessary to carry survival supplies, which include plenty of water.

In his classic, *The Man Who Walked Through Time*, Colin Fletcher describes his two-month walk through the Grand Canyon. Not that we recommend hiking through the Grand Canyon; we mention it as an example of canyon hiking and some of the problems as well as some of the rewards.

Just east of the town of Moab in Utah there is a trail called the Moab Slickrock Bike Trail. This trail, which is strictly a motorcycle trail, traverses an extensive formation of Navajo sandstone, virtually indestructible, called slickrock. Similar bedrock can be used for walking, and if this is the type of terrain in your neck of the woods, here is your linear space.

Finding the Space

Just how do you go out and "discover and use" your own linear space? If it is posted, you should obtain permission to use it. The seeking and finding is as much fun as the using. But what then? You can, of course, keep using it yourself—for walking, jogging or bicycling, as the case may be. You might want to share it with your friends or with your hiking or bicycling club. Or you might want to go further.

What about having it designated as a public recreation-way to be used by the public and perhaps even owned by the public? Now we are talking about a project you or your friends might want to undertake.

Most of the established recreation-ways on rights-of-way are the result of action by some governmental unit—town, county or state—or by an established conservation or recreation group. In some cases private enterprise, such as a utility company or a lumber company, will give the public permission to use private logging roads. As a matter of fact, since we are talking about land which might be privately owned, at some point action by some governmental unit or agency will be necessary if this land is to be placed in the public domain.

Well, then, where do you fit in? The role of the citizen is basically to plant a seed, to petition, to generate interest, and to aid in planning. Even though more and more states, counties, and towns are actively considering the use of abandoned rights-of-way and incorporating them in their recreation planning, the effort is still minimal. Many opportunities have been lost because the facts were not brought to the attention of the appropriate government unit or agency or because no real citizen interest was shown.

This is where you come in. First, find a piece of linear space. Determine its feasibility for walking, bicycling or jogging. Where does it go? Can it be used as a linkage? Do some research on it. Who owns it? When was it abandoned? Is it of historical interest? What has to be done to make it usable? Armed with this information, prepare a plan. Then contact your local bicycling club or hiking club. Contact the local Boy Scout and Girl Scout Councils, the local Rotary club, the Chamber of Commerce. They might be only too glad to offer their services in clearing the trail and in maintaining the trail once established. It is just this offer of help that can get the local municipality interested. Write a letter to the local newspaper—get them behind you. Last, but not least, contact the landowners along the rights-of-way; they might need some reassurance. It is better to have them on your side than against you.

A few case histories of citizen action will give you some idea of what can be done.

Perhaps the most well known is the role that Justice William O. Douglas played in the establishment of the C & O Canal National Historic Park. There were plans to use the canal right-of-way for a highway. In 1954, Justice Douglas led a group which hiked the entire length of the canal. When they arrived in Georgetown, they found a crowd of fifty thousand supporters waiting to greet them. What Justice Douglas had done, basically, was to publicize the danger to the canal and rally support in opposition to the highway. The highway plans were dropped, the canal towpath was designated a hiking and bicycling trail, and eventually the entire canal was declared a National Historic Park.

The Illinois Prairie Path, running along the abandoned Chicago, Aurora and Elgin interurban railway right-of-way, is really the result of one person's stubborn refusal to give up. It can truly be said that Mrs. May Watts really discovered this weed-grown right-of-way. One day in 1963, she was driving along a road near her home and crossed an abandoned railroad right-of-way. She immediately recognized the potential for a trail since she had recently visited England and was impressed with their many public footpaths. She wrote a letter to the *Chicago Tribune* and obtained their support. Considerable interest and support was generated and before long the Illinois Prairie Path group was organized. They were able to get the county to purchase the right-of-way and designate a ten-foot walking path through the right-of-way. The Commonwealth Edison Company shares its power line easements with the path. Most of the right-of-way is policed and maintained by local scout troops and other volunteers.

The New York State Barge Canal, stretching 363 miles across New York State, seems like a natural for a cross-state recreational facility. With commercial tonnage decreasing, it was becoming a recreational waterway. But what about a cross-state linear park? A walkway across the state connecting small mini-parks along the way. One of the first of these mini-parks was the brainchild of Mrs. Mary K. Dischaw of Ogden, New York. With community support and the active participation of scout troops, local garden clubs, Chamber of Commerce members and many other volunteers, a short Tow Path Trail was developed on the state-owned land along the barge canal. This was followed by the Wide Waters Park, a small park adjacent to the canal. But Mary had a greater dream—"Why not do this for the entire length of the canal?" This was in 1968. Since then, other towns along the canal have established similar small parks. The State of New York has built larger parks at some of the locks including an observation platform for viewing the locking through of boats. Sections of the service road have been converted into smooth bicycle paths and there are plans to eventually have a continuous canal trail across the state—truly a cross-state linear park. And Mrs. Dischaw deserves credit for being one of the first to sow the seed.

The last remaining lock of the old Erie Canal in Monroe County, New York, was almost completely hidden from view by dense growth. However, the stonework was still in perfect condition and it occurred to a couple of citizens that this example of America's industrial heritage should be made accessible to the public. This could be done by clearing the towpath to the lock, which would also serve as a link between the barge canal and a town bikeway.

A committee, headed by Mrs. Judy Kaplan of the town of Pittsford, immediately went to work. Working closely with town officials, the New York State Department of Transportation (which held title to the land), the local utility company, Boy Scout and Girl Scout troops, the local Rotary club, an Army Reserve unit, local merchants, and many other interested citizens and volunteers, the committee was able to hold a "Lock 62 Park and Trail" dedication exactly one year from the start of the project. This was due to the superb planning and guidance of a few people, but perhaps more important, it is a remarkable display of how a group of private citizens can work together with local government to accomplish such a goal.

Exploring existing spaces for recreation alternatives will enable you to fill your leisure time with activities that go beyond customary notions of play to the realm of conservation and "re-creation."

chapter 5

The Course

by Ann Buxbaum

Every morning at 6:30, a thirty-five-year-old Boston bank executive emerges from his front door, runs the two blocks to a city park, and jogs around the loop that lies along its edges. Thirty minutes later, he has run 1½ miles and exercised virtually every muscle and joint in his body with the help of twenty simple instructional signs along the trail. He is home in time for breakfast and a leisurely walk to the bus that will take him to work. The only disruption to this pattern is the increasing insistence of his ten-year-old daughter that she come along with him on his run. She used to slow him down, but his pleasure in her company is now doubled by his delight in her growing skill and endurance; he can see the day when she will have to hold back for him!

Several times a week, he stops to chat with a fifty-year-old woman for whom the fitness trail is a new discovery. She thought herself too old for regular running and exercises, but a friend persuaded her to try it one bright spring weekend, and she has become addicted to the activity, claiming that she feels dull and grumpy if she skips more than a day at a time.

Another regular is a twenty-six-year-old teacher, whose easy, loping pace bears witness to her almost lifelong running habit. She doesn't take the time to do the indicated exercises. Instead, she warms up with her own chosen exercises and circles the trail three or four times without stopping. She used to jog on the streets, but when her city built its first fitness trail, the beauty of the woods, the clarity of the air, and the resilient, springy

105

running surface drew her to this kind of running place, and she has become an enthusiastic convert.

Later in the morning, you may find a young mother making her first tentative approach to jogging and exercise, while keeping one eye on her preschooler in the adjacent playground.

A couple in their seventies walks briskly the length of the loop, jogging a bit here and there, and doing all the prescribed exercises with remarkable agility and obvious zest.

A group of local firefighters shows up at lunch-time; they are conditioning themselves by regular use of the trail in order to keep their bodies tuned for the immense demands of their work.

Other lunch-time users appear—a pair of secretaries, a university student, a businessman.

In the late afternoon, you will see schoolchildren and adolescents, some seriously training themselves for athletics or general endurance, and some just enjoying the equipment and the pleasure of letting off steam with some hard running. On pleasant summer days, the hours of use stretch into the late evening, and on weekends, whole families will gather to toss a frisbee, picnic, fish, play softball, and try their hand at the fitness trail.

Clearly, the fitness trail is for play, and its simple signs, rustic path, and sturdy, functional wooden exercise stations qualify as low technology. But it is a playspace with a difference; it has been carefully designed to create and maintain the health of the heart and lungs of those who use it regularly, and to foster flexibility and muscle strength as well.

Need for Trails

Why should it be necessary to construct such trails? Don't most Americans spend much of their lives "running around?" Look at the people lined up for two hours waiting at the local tennis courts. Look at the health spas, where, for several hundred dollars a year, you can use the most complicated machinery to trim, slim, and shape up. Look at the golf courses, with hundreds of people waiting to tee off on a sunny day. Look at the snow shovelers, the lawn mowers. . . .

But perhaps you have already seen the fallacies in these arguments. "Running around" usually translates to "driving around," accumulating packages, dropping off or picking up

5-1: The Handwalk.

5-2: The Balance Beam.

children. Weekend tennis often means an intensely stressful, competitive hour of "play"; or conversely, standing in one spot and patting the ball gently over the net, rarely moving and never exerting oneself for more than a few moments. Health spas, restricted to those with leisure and money, often emphasize "spot reducing" or "muscle building," and show little concern for the energetic, sustained, gradually-increasing activity that is necessary to promote genuine good health. Golfers may get in some walking, but more and more, they are actually not *permitted* to walk on the course, being forced to use a golf cart to keep the greens from being trampled by human feet! Snow is shoveled by men (mostly) whose bodies are not conditioned for the tremendous strain that the activity puts on their hearts; if they choose to avoid the well-known dangers of such sporadic, intense demands on the body, they resort to a snow-blower. And a power mower.

And so it goes. For most working people, life consists of driving to a job; sitting all day, except for time out for coffee and a Danish or a quick lunch; driving home; slumping exhausted in front of the television set until bedtime. The boredom and dreariness of this routine is spiced by frequent consoling drinks, heavy, fat-laden meals, cigarettes to calm us down, and endless cups of coffee to charge us up. For women who are still at home, the routine is likely to include some physical activity—pushing a vacuum cleaner, carrying clothes and dishes from place to place, making beds—but it is tedious, and too limited to keep them alert, healthy, and fit.

For children, there is, of course, a greater opportunity for energetic motion: outdoor play is still an important part of their lives. But society is doing its best to discourage even our children from what comes so naturally to them. School often consists of six or more hours of sitting, and organized athletics are geared only to the elite few. Parents feel obligated to drive their children almost everywhere, and television is more and more taking over their leisure time.

Seventeen percent of American children are clinically obese, a combination of their appalling eating habits and the lack of activity in their lives. The latter is probably the more crucial factor; many medical studies have shown that obese youngsters actually eat less than their thin friends, but they expend far fewer calories in the normal course of their day.

We are all familiar with these patterns, and to some extent, most of us recognize some part of our own lives in them. But this discouraging picture is not unique to the United States. To a great extent, it is the underside of the coin of affluence, and industrialized societies all over the world are beginning to recognize it as a broad social and medical problem. The tremendous increase in labor-saving devices, automobiles, television, and sedentary work has been accompanied by a concomitant increase in cardiovascular disease. Diet and smoking habits surely play a great part, and must also be dealt with by the individual concerned with his or her health, or the country concerned with the health of its citizens. But the lack of exercise in our daily lives is equally important, and there is some evidence that a program of physical fitness makes people feel better about their bodies, decreasing the insecurity and tension that lead to overeating and smoking.

5-3: The Hip Swing.

Courses in Europe

Some countries are way ahead of us in their recognition that regular exercise is an effective intervening force in unhealthy lifestyles. Two pioneers are Sweden and Switzerland, both of which have created miles of walking-jogging trails throughout their cities, towns, and countryside. The Swedes encourage people by a carefully planned program of physical education, beginning with the very youngest children and continuing as long as people live. Schools, community centers, supermarkets, industries, and facilities for the aged and the handicapped all foster the maintenance of physical fitness. Because of a twenty-five-year effort to involve people in their own health, the concept has become almost universally accepted, and the woodland trails are heavily used at all times of the day and night, with lights along many of them to facilitate running and skiing through the long Swedish autumns and winters.

The Swiss have designed a network of exercise facilities which also encourage jogging or hiking along forest paths, but they have formalized their exercise opportunities by spacing signs along the path, with pictures and descriptions of prescribed exercises, many of them using simple equipment located next to the signs. The Vita Insurance Company has acted as initiator and sponsor of the system, and the Parcours Vita is to be found in virtually every city and town across the country—more than 450 in all.

The logic of the fitness trail, whether the varied, unstructured Swedish model, or the more highly organized Swiss version, is based on the proven physical benefits of aerobic exercise. Such exercise is designed to increase endurance—the effective functioning of the heart and lungs. Fast walking, running, cross-country skiing, biking, jumping rope, and swimming are the best aerobic activities.

By definition, aerobics demands consistent, steady motion, maintained for about thirty minutes at a rate individually determined to strengthen the heart muscle without overstressing it. Simply jogging or walking briskly for a half hour three times a week offers an adequate amount of stimulation to the heart; adding such exercises as deep knee bends, head movements, swings, pulls, pushes, and jumps brings agility and looseness to

5-4: The Log Jump.

muscles and joints, helping ease or avoid stiffness, tension, and joint pain.

More and more Americans, having had the chance to travel abroad, have experienced the pleasures of the Swiss Parcours Vita, the Swedish training track, and similar facilities in other European countries. Some have brought the fitness trail concept back to their hometowns or university campuses, and several versions have begun to spring up in various parts of the United States. Where well designed and carefully built, fitness trails have proven very popular, attracting a wide range of users, particularly among those who had never found it convenient or pleasant to exercise before.

As the movement has spread across the country, several variations have developed. Commercial and non-profit companies offer packages of station signs and equipment specifications and blue-prints, which purchasers may use in putting together their own fiitness trails, according to their particular needs and location. Some schools and universities have built trails without buying packages, often using student designs, but generally taking off from the Swiss model.

A few enterprising individuals have even constructed their own trails for personal and family use. Robert McCaldon, M.D., D.Psych., of Kingston, Ontario, has done it this way: using his own farm, he has taken advantage of the rolling hills, rocks, trees, and ponds to devise twenty simple but strenuous exercises. There is a chinning bar wedged into the limbs of two trees. There is a knotted rope hanging from a branch. There is a rock for step-ups, a log for running across the pond, a hill to run up backwards. Despite some suggested adaptations for the less fit or experienced, Dr. McCaldon's invention is designed primarily for the confirmed runner and exerciser, with a most imaginative and virtually cost-free combination of path and equipment.

In Boston, Friedrich Schneider, an instructor in Health Dynamics at Boston University, has done much the same thing, but using the city streets, stairs, railroad tracks, fences, and con-crete barriers for the exercises. He can lay out a fitness trail in virtually any neighborhood by scanning the existing structures and devising a half-hour run that encompasses several which can be climbed on, jumped across, pushed against, or run along. Once again, his scheme is probably best suited to the fitness enthusiast

5-5: The Situp.

who does not need the organized path, the prescribed exercises, and the informative signs to motivate and instruct. Certainly there is a kind of voluntary simplicity to any exercise or play activity that does not require equipment.

Despite the variety of approaches and cost, the keynotes of all fitness trails are simplicity, physiological benefits, and *fun!* In many ways, this last is the most important factor; clearly, the most beautifully designed, health-giving program is a failure if it does not appeal to a lot of people over a long period of time. Thus the woods, or interesting city streets: cool, fresh, traffic-free, changing with the seasons. Thus the equipment: simple enough for a small child or an older person, but challenging enough for

5-6: The Vault.

the physical fitness enthusiast. Thus, the exercise stations: a base from which to increase one's agility and endurance, to progress from breathless straining to ease and confidence.

Running the Course

What kinds of exercises will you find along a fitness trail? Again, despite a large variety of choices, the progression is usually similar, from warm-ups through more strenuous conditioners to the final cooling down.

The warm-ups often require no equipment; they emphasize flexibility and looseness. Swings of arms and legs, shoulder rolls, muscle stretches are all valuable preparations for running and help dissipate the tightness that can lead to discomfort and pain. They are, in addition, easy to do and encouraging for the new jogger. With regular practice, flexibility can increase startlingly in a very short time.

The central core of exercises is generally designed to increase coordination and strength, and is far more challenging to the novice. This group may include sit-ups, jumps of different kinds, hanging and pulling from bars, ladders, or rings, and push-ups. These tend to focus on the upper body and to require more strength than the first group. Most beginners are encouraged to do only a few of each exercise, working up gradually to the suggested number of repetitions.

Usually the kinds of exercise in this group alternate from simple to more difficult, from abdominal to neck and shoulders, from pushing to pulling. The alternation makes the whole sequence complementary and adds to the pleasure and variety.

The last segment of most fitness trails is for winding down, and often suggests walking the last several yards of the course. The process is sometimes aided by a station such as the balance beam, which forces the user to move slowly and deliberately, concentrating on fine muscle control. At the end of this sequence, the body has cooled off and become relaxed, and the transition from exertion to rest has been neatly built into the sequence. It is important to remember that, though the various stations show specific exercises, how you travel the circuit is really up to you. I have seen people literally dance around the course. So,

5-7: The Run.

even though there are prescribed exercises, you are really on
your own to invent, to play, to improvise.

In Sweden, at the beginning and end of many running loops,
you will find a Trim Centre. This is an attractive building, blending with the surrounding woods or fields, and offering showers
and saunas, changing rooms, and small restaurants; the Swedes
see exercise as a social activity and stress the rewards of a friendly
snack after a hard run!

Some centres also offer exercise rooms as an alternative to
stations along the actual running path. And some include a
facility with trained technicians for annual cardiovascular stress
testing. This is a procedure which offers a precise measurement
of the reaction of individual bodies to controlled amounts of
graduated exercise. It is useful in figuring out how much aerobic
activity will condition a given person, and at what point the heart
will be working as hard as it safely can. It is also valuable as a

measure of one's progress over the years, and is a strong encouragement to maintain a pattern of regular exercise.

I have not been able to find any American equivalent of the Trim Centre, except in some industries which provide elegant and expensive eating and working-out facilities for top executives. If executives can use it, ordinary citizens should find it just as appealing, and we may well see inexpensive, pleasant, convenient centers spring up in conjunction with fitness trails, encouraging the users to relax, chat, shower, eat, and socialize together. The point is that play and recreation should be a social activity; not one in which new records are sought but one in which we can explore new dimensions of ourselves in concert with others.

Planning the Course

Once you have been convinced that a fitness trail is a good idea, how do you get started? The process is, of course, totally different from community to community, but the general requirements are the same: enough land; easy access; enough shade to provide relief from summer sun; and adequate drainage to prevent puddles or swamps.

Public parks make wonderful sites for fitness trails, because they are already established as a focus of activity. Where other recreational facilities exist—picnic areas, playgrounds, baseball diamonds, tennis courts—a fitness trail becomes easily visible to large numbers of people and attracts new users all the time.

In northern Europe, you find such trails, as often as not, in fairly remote areas, with nothing much around them except fields and woods. To locate an American trail in such an isolated setting would perhaps result in minimal use, at least until the idea gains wider acceptance and a public exists who will go out of their way to find and use such a facility.

This does not, of course, eliminate developing remote areas with several new facilities at the same time. Hiking and walking trails, wildlife museums, and picnic spaces will draw groups of people and create the kind of atmosphere in which a fitness trail will thrive.

Conservationists all over the country are looking for ways to bring people into open land without destroying its beauty, and

5-8: The Rest.

such low-key, multipurpose development would seem ideal. More than one conservation area has been transformed from an isolated, unsightly dump to a community playspace. As you have seen in the previous chapter, there exist countless unused linear paths across the country which could serve as sites for exercise trails.

As in any community project, no matter how apparently simple, each case is slightly different. The leaders in the community, the sources of funding, the lay of the land, the prevailing lifestyles—all have a considerable effect on the progress and obstacles that will mark the construction of a fitness trail.

Backyard Trails

There are many alternatives for individuals and communities who desire to "construct" trails on their own. The most simple course would probably be the kind that Friedrich Schneider "invents" for himself in the streets of Boston. He discovers his exercise stations as he goes along. For him, recreation comes from the existing environment.

In his words, "Nature can be our playground. Children find joy in every tree; they find activity in every rock along the way. They don't try to avoid a ditch; rather they run through it or jump over it. To children the natural environment presents no obstacles. They transform everything in their path into play objects—sources of recreation and delight."

According to Schneider, we merely have to look around us to consider "ways to play." We have to consider trees and rocks and stairs and walls as instruments of play and exercise.

He believes that "there's no reason to spend money when everything you need for a fitness trail is all around you. You want to do sit-ups, sit in the grass, sit in a baseball field. Don't worry about people watching you.

"Make your own fitness trail. I have one on which I take my students. We use whatever we find along the way. On rocks we can do sit-ups or step-ups. On railings or ledges we do press-ups or zig-zag jumps.

"My God, a playground is the perfect exercise system and there are playgrounds everywhere."

So consider your own community, whether it's in a town, city, or suburban area. Is there a convenient place to walk and run close to home? Once you have determined this, think about the exercise and play possibilities "along the way." Railroad tracks and low walls to balance on. What about the curb itself, which children love to use for their balancing games? Are there steps to climb, obstacles to "frog leap" over, low branches for pull-ups, logs and rocks to lift, markers on telephone poles to jump for, sidewalk cracks to hopscotch through, and so on?

If you make your neighborhood your course, you can work countless variations on this basic pattern. And, with some ingenuity, you can bring the play indoors (zig-zag through the living room and then do fifteen leapfrogs). There is, in Schneider's opinion, nothing childish about this. "Inventing neighborhood trails can be a spontaneous activity which brings out the play in all of us. Don't worry about people watching you."

5-9: The Stairs.
(By permission of the *Boston Herald American*)

5-10: The Tracks.
(By permission of the *Boston Herald American*)

Perhaps you want a more permanent type of trail in your community, complete with signs at the various stations. If so, Schneider suggests, although you could probably do the work on your own, that you go through your local Parks and Recreation Department which will be familiar with available sites.

Once you have found a site, it would be helpful for you to get a topographical map from the town engineer to aid you in preparing a course according to elevations, natural obstacles, boundaries, and existing trails. Schneider, who approaches the planning of a course from the point of view of a naturalist, tries to leave the environment as undisturbed as possible.

Accordingly, he uses the natural environment for various exercises. Rocks and benches to aid in sit-ups. Fallen trees for push-ups. Trees with branches at different heights or telephone poles with markings at different heights for squat jumps. Logs or rocks for frog jumps. Trees with sturdy branches for pull-ups. Marked trees for zig-zag runs. Logs for balancing.

Schneider adds very little apparatus. He recommends different colored arrows indicating walk, jog, run, and sprint. He constructs his station markers, which outline the name and position of the exercise, out of marine plywood. The figures and the exercise names can be burned, painted or routed directly on the wood.

Schneider suggests that a town could change its course regularly with the help of the media. Biweekly or monthly changes might be announced in the newspaper. It would simply mean changing the stations, thus adding to the variety of the game.

He is confident that the people can discover a playspace in the natural world without disturbing anything. "Give me," he boasts, "the entire Charles River (Boston) and I could find two hundred exercise stations without any problem."

While the idea of "inventing the course" might appeal to some, perhaps you want to establish a "fixed" course in your own backyard or in conjunction with some of your neighbors. If so, you could get at no cost the "Parcours Handbook" from the Bureau of Outdoor Recreation (Technical Assistance Division, BOR Pacific Southwest Regional Office, P.O. Box 36062, San Francisco, California 94102), which provides construction details and suggestions for the various stations.

Anatomy of Some Courses

Creating a course in your own backyard is a fairly simple thing to do. Consider the case of Dr. McCaldon, who decided to construct a course on his own land. He reports that "apart from the knotted rope and iron bar, all the exercise stations were constructed with natural materials lying about on the course. For example, a military press is done with a log or a rock, triceps press and step-up are both done on large, square boulders, and an excellent quadriceps exercise is obtained by running up a grassy slope backwards. The signs were hand-drawn with a felt-tip pen on scrap boards. Plywood is unsuitable, as the porcupines eat it. The trail was marked with discarded plastic primer trays left over from shot-shell reloading. These were tacked to trees or to stakes in the ground. The trail needs a once-over in the spring to remove fallen branches, and a rough cutting with a scythe about midsummer.

"Although the course can be as varied and as imaginative as terrain and equipment will permit, I'll describe mine as a representative example.

"One hundred meters along a set of tractor tracks is the first station, step-up on a rock, ten times for each leg.

"The path winds down into a valley of grass. Number two is a push-up, ten repetitions. The hardier may put their feet uphill for this exercise, vice versa for women and children.

"Three is a horizontal arm fling, ten each side, to stretch out the pectorals used in the previous exercise.

"Now the trail enters a wooded valley, and, as the ground rises, there is a steel bar wedged in the limbs of two trees. This is the chin-up, eight repetitions. Those who can't do it can substitute three 'skin-the-cats.'

"Number five is only fifty meters away, and demands fifty partial sit-ups.

"The path crosses the end of this field, winds through a narrow ridge of hardwoods where number six is located, the alternate toe touch.

"The trail then enters some mixed, rough terrain of rocks, hardwoods, hemlocks and open spaces along the length of a beaver pond. Number seven is a climb up to the top of a knotted rope tied to a high branch in an old oak tree.

5-11: The Obstacle.
(By permission of the *Boston Herald American*)

5-12 through 5-14: Backyard course in Kingston, Ontario.

"Number eight is a set of deep knee bends. Logs are provided to place across the shoulders and add some weight to the exercise.

"The trail then crosses a narrow part of the beaver pond on a log. It must be crossed boldly and surely or the runner will find his shoes full of swampy water! Scramble up a hill, and there, amidst a stand of graceful beech trees, one finds number nine, the stride jump.

"The next run is the longest, some six hundred meters along the far side of the beaver pond. Here the trail is dark and thick with hemlocks, then light and sun-spattered through young growth of hard maples. Number ten keeps the heart and lungs working, for it is ten repetitions of a squat-thrust.

"The path skirts the end of the pond, crosses a footbridge and arrives at the base of a rocky cliff, where there is a leg and calf exercise called "jump-up." It is simply two brief hops, crouch until the hands touch the ground, then spring upwards with as much force as possible. Ten repetitions are enough to wear you out at this stage.

"The next station, number twelve, consists of running up an open slope backwards. This uses the powerful quadriceps muscles at the front of the thigh, the opposite of the hamstrings used in usual running.

"And on it goes, covering twenty stations in all. The course ends with a hundred-meter run.

"The path was chosen to go around as many obstacles as possible. Some ax work in the spring and some hacking with a serrated, two-edged scythe in midsummer maintain the trail. Fluorescent tape on tree limbs, or stakes pounded into the ground can also serve as markers. A rough sign, drawn with a felt-tip, indelible pen and using stick figures, explains the exercise at each station. This usually needs relettering once every year. Crude board is best. The porcupines demolish any tasty plywood that is pinned up. Thus, maintenance is exceedingly easy.

"Of course, my list of exercises is by no means exhaustive. There are many more, especially of a stretching kind, which may be done with little or no paraphernalia."

The Parcours trail can double as a nature walk for three seasons of the year, and a cross-country ski trail in the winter.

Other individuals have constructed abbreviated trails to conform to smaller land areas. With the help of the local Boy Scouts,

Charles Brown, Director of the Department of Parks and Recreation, Bethlehem, Pennsylvania, designed and built eight exercise stations adjacent to an existing footpath.

Brown thought of the idea while walking along the trail. "We are blessed to have this area," he said to himself. "This is an ideal spot for family recreation."

With Robert Rowe, who was working for his Eagle honor badge, Brown hiked along the trail noting the possibilities in the lush and aged forest. Together they discovered the best locations for the stations.

Material was readily available. The Boy Scouts gleaned lumber from the local telephone company and discarded signs from the traffic department.

Rowe spent forty hours walking back and forth, deciding how to best integrate an abbreviated physical fitness trail into the park. Even a massive water tower became an asset as it makes the station easier to locate. Rowe, with the aid of his troop, spent an additional forty hours preparing the station signs, widening the trail, and installing the equipment.

While less elaborate than many fitness trails, the Bethlehem course is perfectly adequate for the one-acre site.

Evolution of a Trail

In Newton, Massachusetts, a fitness trail was developed largely through the efforts of one committed citizen, who then mobilized a battery of people and services to implement his idea. About four years ago, this man visited Sweden, Finland, and Switzerland, and came home tremendously enthusiastic about the outdoor fitness facilities he had seen and used in all three countries. He saw no reason why his home town could not use some of its parkland to create a similar facility, and he embarked on a year-long effort to make it happen.

The first several months were spent talking with citizen groups and appearing at formal meetings of the recreation commission and the board of aldermen. At these meetings, he would show his homemade slides of wooded running paths and exercise stations, trying to convey some of the pleasures of these trails to people who had never heard of the concept. After nearly a year, the recreation commission agreed to commit an existing park site and $2,000 to construct the first fitness trail in the area.

The layout of the path and location of equipment were planned and supervised by an architect who didn't even live in the city, but found the growing enthusiasm contagious. The lumber was supplied and cut at cost by a playground equipment firm. A nearby consulting organization provided several volunteers to work on the actual construction, and remained intimately involved with all the details of the project.

Notices in local newspapers yielded many city residents who made up the work crew during the five weekends it took to complete the job. Children joined their parents, and amateur carpenters would show up with hammers, saws, and levels. A student in landscape architecture oversaw all the work sessions and revised the plans when unforeseen New England rock beds or unmapped water pipes were encountered.

About halfway through the project, some local teenagers who considered the park their "turf" began to show curiosity about all the activity. They were asked once or twice to help move particularly heavy rocks, or to hammer a pole into the ground. Gradually, they became part of the crew and expressed interest in the exercise stations that they were now helping to build.

One of the volunteers, a skilled gymnastics teacher, gave them a special tour of the trail, suggesting extra exercises they could do to challenge themselves beyond the requirements of the signs, and to prove their prowess. Several of these young people later became unofficial protectors of "their" fitness trail, and some of them have even turned into periodic joggers!

The original facility used existing access roads and unimproved paths through the woods. Despite the potholes, roots, and broken limbs, use of the trail surpassed the expectations of even the earliest optimists. On a pleasant Sunday as many as two hundred people might show up, and even on ordinary weekdays, a steady stream of regular users could be counted on in all kinds of weather.

This unexpected success stimulated the recreation commission to install a genuine running path about a year after the original construction, and they appropriated $6,000 to do so. The new path, now in use for a year, has required virtually no maintenance, and use of the trail has continued steadily, so that the city is hoping to construct another one.

Alternatives

Since the purpose of this book is to emphasize low-cost recreation alternatives, you are encouraged to invent your own course with as little expense as possible. There are other options, however.

The J. C. Penney Company will supply a trail kit, without cost, to any community where there is a J. C. Penney retail store or a local Jaycees service club which elects to participate in the program. The local Penney retail store may assist financially with the trail construction and the Jaycees club may provide the labor to get the trail on the ground. The trail kit consists of a set of sixty-five signs and the necessary instructions for developing the trail.

In a community without either a Penney retail store or a Jaycees club, the Penney company will provide the materials, at cost (approximately $150), to the community.

For complete details you should contact the local J. C. Penney store manager or Mr. James C. Schwaninger, Public Relations, J. C. Penney Company, Inc., 1301 Avenue of the Americas, New York, New York 10019.

Finally, there are a number of companies listed in the Appendix that sell course kits which usually include a set of signs, blueprints for building the exercise equipment and the specifications for clearing and properly grooming the trail.

chapter 6

The Bike

by James C. McCullagh

As you have seen in chapters four and five, we are surrounded by useable and reuseable space which, like a pleasure grid, waits for our attention. Linear space for our good feet and good wheels.

Canals, towpaths, and railroad beds, whose historic uses turn up memories, are sources and sites of recreation—often waiting to be discovered. And many of these spaces call out for the bike—a perfect marriage of efficient machine and efficient use of space.

The bike. That strange and wonderful machine which is said to have sprung fully loaded and designed from the mind of Leonardo da Vinci. The bike. That design of grace and wonder which became aesthetic when the ball bearing came along. The bike. Perhaps the ultimate machine.

Look around you on Sunday afternoon most weeks of the year. Bikes are part of the background scenario against which the rest of the community moves. Invade the parks and trails and watch the bikes hum effortlessly against the green of the day.

The Way

Look at some popular magazine ads and you will often see the bike resting in the cool and sensuous underbrush of spring.

Or on television, a road racer cycles home to the tune of a microwave oven. Or in Washington, D.C., a congressman straddles his bike on camera proclaiming that this machine is the ideal transportation alternative. Or in Seattle, Washington, Paul

MacCready invents a pedal-power plane, renewing old beliefs that our legs can take us anywhere.

To call the bike the perfect machine, the ultimate in recreation accompaniment, is not hyperbole. It raises recreation to the consummate level. On the bike you can go anywhere, from around the block to around the world.

The bicycle might be considered the democratic machine since it can be used universally by young and old, by adult and child, by man and woman. All can participate equally, fraternally in bike-centered recreation activities.

The bicycle can be thought of as recreation in search of recreation. A simple bicycle ride, even if it's just around the neighborhood, can provide pleasure and well-being; and, for many, a heightening of consciousness. On the other hand, cycling also enables us to get to other recreation sites and activities. And, since the range of the bike is limited only by the desire and hardiness of the participants, this machine brings many forms of recreation to our doorsteps.

At a time when family recreation is more difficult to find, the bicycle stands as a splendid opportunity for family sport. Rather than splintering off into various pursuits requiring different levels of ability and commitment, cyclists of all ages and genders can participate as a unit at a level and pace all can enjoy.

For those people who enjoy active recreation but don't like to engage in competition, the bicycle is the answer. At its best, cycling can be a rejuvenating non-competitive sport.

In an age when actual participation in sports ends for many after high school and college, the bicycle offers a challenge and opportunity for lifetime enjoyment, for a lifesport that will offer over the years experiences as varied as the seasons.

The bicycle is one of the few machines that can move us unobtrusively within the environment. The bicycle can be nestled in the deep, rich glow of the forest and nothing will be changed, not the contour of the land, not the afternoon cry of the blue jay.

The bicycle is the modern recreation tool, as it allows us to practice and pursue our interest in adventure. Since we are essentially mobile creatures, the bicycle complements our need for movement, and allows us to reach out like restless ambassadors, to discover and appreciate new communities in a way not customarily described in travel brochures. The bicycle allows us

6-1: The Capital Area Greenway, Raleigh, North Carolina.

to slow down sufficiently to discover the rich, human space that communities are.

Perhaps there is no finer way to recreate ourselves than with the bicycle, recreate ourselves through assuming control of our mobility, recreate ourselves through the physical joy the bicycle delivers, and recreate ourselves through the comradeship and goodwill of our fellow "travelers."

As some cyclists like to believe, God created bicycles and then created roads to carry them. Of course, cyclists don't pedal on thin air. They travel on the brunt and roar of American roads. For this reason many individuals and communities across the nation have felt it their responsibility to create appropriate spaces

6-2: The Third Creek Bicycle Trail, Knoxville, Tennessee.

6-3

6-4

6-3 through 6-5:
The Bicycle in Davis,
California.
(Courtesy of Cindy O'Dell)

6-5

for the cyclists. For those who believe in self-generated and self-maintained community spaces, the bicycle trail has become a priority item.

The Space

In the final chapter of *Ways to Play*, Malcolm Wells writes, buoyantly and optimistically, that "someday, perhaps during our lifetimes, if the life-movement continues its lusty growth, the towns and cities of America will be all vine-draped and meadowed and ready for healthy outdoor play." While few cities in this country seem "ready for healthy outdoor play," Davis, California, with the bicycle the center of its personality, comes very close.

Davis has a population of 30,000 and has 25,000 bicycles. Since the late 1960s, the city has developed, largely at the insistence of its citizens, a bicycle network that is unrivaled in the United States. James Ridgeway notes that "it is important to realize that bicycles are not merely owned, stored, or used for recreational purposes; they are an important part of the transportation system. On one heavily traveled street, traffic counts during the summer showed that bicycles represented 40 percent of all traffic. During the rush hour, 90 percent of all riders are adult."

The bicycle has definitely aided in the "greening" of Davis. With the bicycle came shade trees, energy conservation, recycling, cottage industries, and the like. For Davis the bicycle is a quintessential ingredient in its quest for low-technology living.

Clearly we can't all do what Davis has done, but we can work to make the bicycle an actual and symbolic presence in the community. We can "discover" and "construct" within our community spaces where the bicycle is welcome. We can, like Ann Calagaz of Mobile, Alabama, mobilize our community and cycle to city hall with two thousand people and ask for bike trails in the city. Or we can, like Ann Calagaz and her husband, help map trails between communities. To the Calagaz family, there is recreation in such an adventure.

"My husband and I," Ann Calagaz reports, "were asked to help map a part of the Bartram Trail (from Mobile to the Florida state line). One Sunday we were riding through, taking turns on bike and car. Somewhere west of Greenville, Alabama, I was

6-6: Opening of first highway-marked bicycle route in Alabama. Ann Calagaz, trailblazer.

riding along on a beautiful country road. There was no fencing, no telephone or electric wires. The landscape was just lovely with the hills sloping down to a country stream and a farmhouse over in the woods when an old man in a rocking chair said to me, 'Hey lady, what are you doing on *my road?*' When I told him I was from Mobile, he replied, 'Bet you are plumb tuckered out.' He wanted to know my name and all my relatives and he asked me if I would like to sit down a spell and rest my weary bones. As I traveled further down the road, there was a family cutting watermelon and they hollered out, 'Won't you stop and have some?' "

While it might be difficult for individuals to actually "construct" bike trails, it is not at all difficult for them to help in mapping out trails on existing roads in order to encourage more cycling.

According to James J. Berryhill, who is probably the country's leading expert on bicycle trails, the Rutherford County

(Tennessee) trail is an excellent example of how facilities can be provided at low cost.

After a series of meetings to determine public support and need for the proposed system the committee used county road maps to mark down a first draft route. One of the objectives of this route was to create a roughly circular routing near the county boundaries. Spoke routes would radiate from the centrally located county seat to this outer route. Another objective considered was the routing of the cyclist to as many natural and historic sites as possible. A third and most important objective was to select the safest possible routes. Busy roads and intersections were avoided. The personal knowledge of local citizens concerning historic and natural sites as well as road conditions, dangerous areas and other information was invaluable. After the initial work map was finished the committee had on paper the basis for a 225-mile bicycle touring system.

Next came the very necessary step of field reconnaissance of the roads on the working map to determine their suitability for bicycle use. The committee quickly determined that many of the roads selected were not appropriate for bicycling. Some were not paved while others carried high volumes of traffic. Other routes were not aesthetically pleasing. As the problems arose the committee went back to the maps to find alternative routes around the problem. Thus an important "give and take" process developed by which the actual route selected was an evolutionary descendant of the original proposed routes, a process that will likely be necessary in the planning of any long-range system.

The initial field surveys were made by automobile in order to speed the process. *However, the final selection was made on the basis of the routes being ridden by bicycle by local student volunteers. This is an important point as no bicycle route should be selected unless it has been surveyed by bicycle!* After this bicycle reconnaissance was completed the final bikeway map was drafted and a special county bikeway map was designed for public distribution.

While the maps were being prepared for public distribution the county marked the routes using stencils made from guides furnished for this purpose. Road intersections were given particular consideration in this marking program.

After opening the system public response has been quite satisfactory with both groups and individuals using the system frequently. An important point in this example is that the entire planning process took less than three months and costs for the entire system were less than $5,000.

Not only semirural areas such as Rutherford County can benefit from this system but highly urbanized areas as well. A case in point is the city of Hapeville near Atlanta, Georgia. Hapeville lies near the Atlanta International Airport and is so highly developed that there are only two vacant lots left in the city. While the city is relatively small, there was concern that something should be done to encourage the use of the bicycle both for children going to school and for general recreation riding.

Tom McCord, a city councilman, spurred the drive for creation of a bicycle facility. The councilman had originally seen the project as a short trail in the city's only major park. Fortunately, however, he contacted the local bicycle club whose members explained how the city's less-used streets could be designated so as to create a self-help system of some 5½ miles in length. The planning steps were similar to those followed in the Rutherford County project. First a special committee was created with local officials and cyclists providing ideas. This committee designated a tentative route which was surveyed by automobile.

During this survey phase several problems were noted, particularly a difficult crossing of the railroad at a traffic-filled crossing and a large number of left-hand turns on the one-way routing that was being proposed. A city recreation official made the casual suggestion that the route direction should be reversed and 90 percent of the left-hand turns were eliminated! *Investigation of the area by bicycle turned up the incredible discovery of a combination bicycle and pedestrian ramp still left from some earlier, more pro-bicycle time which allowed for an easy crossing of the railroad.* The ramp was somewhat weathered but it still was quite functional and had particular utility since it forced the cyclist to dismount and walk the bicycle up the ramp and across the railroad rather than attempting a more dangerous mounted crossing.

The revised routing was surveyed by several bicyclists and further minor changes were made to improve the system. After selection of the final version city engineering personnel marked the system using stencils prepared by Councilman McCord's son. The City Engineer, Joe Hindman, made an important contribution by the addition of further stenciled signs. One of these signs was a "grate" warning sign to caution the cyclist as to the location of dangerous parallel storm water gratings which might cause accidents. A stencil was developed also to caution cyclists to change into lower gears in anticipation of a steep hill with a stop sign at its beginning. The entire stenciling process took two days to accomplish. At the same time a number of yellow diamond signs were installed and a short section of separate bicycle path constructed at the railroad crossing. Additionally, a four-foot-wide bicycle lane was painted on the three most heavily traveled streets near the airport itself as a safety measure.

The system has proven to be a valuable addition to the city's resources, accomplished at a total cost of less than $500 and less than a week's worth of work by the city engineering crews.

The preceding examples clearly show that the bicycle activist, through cooperation with local officials and clubs, can extend the riding space in his community. Perhaps there is no better example of an individual taking charge of his own recreation.

The Tour

Of course, discovering cycling areas in your community is just one form of recreation. For many, a more enjoyable kind is the bicycle tour, which, as you will see in the following first-person accounts, constitutes more than recreation. For these people, touring has become a lifestyle. As these examples demonstrate, on the bicycle tour you create and define your own riding space.

A. Pete Kutschenreuter

In the summer of 1970, my wife and I bought our first new bicycles since childhood. They were "complicated" five-speed machines with "hand" brakes that took some getting used to. At first we had difficulty learning to shift them when going up steep hills, and we initially reverted to pedaling backwards to brake when going downhill, as had been the procedure for the coaster brake bicycles of our youth.

At first we rode a five-mile leisurely loop each evening, coasting into our driveway at the end of the ride feeling mentally refreshed and pleasantly tired. Within a few weeks we were stretching the distance to ten and then fifteen miles, because those original five miles had become just too short to bother with. One weekend we packed a lunch and went a whole thirty-five miles! After that we were really hooked on bicycling. Since the longer distances meant more time away from home, we installed child carriers on the back of our bicycles, and in 1971 Curt, then age two, and Kathleen, not yet one year old, began to share the scenes and adventures of bicycling with us. They really enjoyed it!

By bicycling each weekend we quickly became experts on the choice secondary roads in our own and neighboring counties, working out routes to the many parks, local airports, restaurants, etc. within a fifty-mile radius of our home. My "baptism" into bicycling maintenance and repair occurred alongside one of these rural roads about thirty-five miles from home. My wife, Bonnie, read the step-by-step instructions from our bicycle owners pamphlet as I apprehensively removed my rear wheel, patched the punctured inner tube, and then replaced the wheel—all in the rain. I then quickly learned what a simple and wonderful machine the bicycle really is, in that it is quite easy to repair and maintain yourself. Gone forever were my fears of venturing out too far from home or from a bicycle shop, for now I was confident that I could take care of the infrequent road repairs that might arise.

Soon thereafter we joined a local bicycle club and our weekend tours further stretched to sometimes fifty and a hundred miles a day. In the spring of 1973 Bonnie and I planned our great adventure. In late June of that year, at age thirty-seven, having been granted a leave of absence from work and with the children happily seated in the child carriers, we pedaled 2,700 miles from Everett, Washington, across the mountains and plains back home to Loveland, Ohio. It had to be the most wonderful family experience in our lifetime. We bicycled about sixty-five miles a day, inhaled the breathtaking scenery, and camped out, frequently under the stars. The people that we met en route couldn't have been nicer or more hospitable. During our last campfire, with the end of the trip at hand, Bonnie and I became a little melancholy as we reminisced about some of the memorable experiences the cross-country trip had brought us. It was then that Curt touchingly said, "Dad, this sure is a great country, someday let's do it again when I can ride my own bicycle."

6-7: Bonnie and Kathleen cycling through rangeland in Montana.

6-8: Curt, Kathleen, and Pete enter Wyoming.

6-9: Curt, Kathleen, and Bonnie pause near the Tetons before climbing to the Continental Divide.

6-10: Bonnie and Kathleen climb Stevens Pass, Washington.

Upon returning from our cross-country adventure, Curt soloed on his own two-wheeler, and later pedaled his small bicycle fifty miles in one day at age six and a hundred miles in one day at age seven. Not to be outdone, a few weeks after her own sixth birthday, Kathleen also pedaled the same small bicycle fifty miles in one day. Bicycling had truly become a family affair for all of us now.

Most of the year, our weekends seem to revolve around bicycling. We enjoy the freedom and independence that recreational bicycling offers, as well as the excellent health it produces. The physical exercise derived, however, is a byproduct of being outside enjoying nature with the fellowship of congenial bicycling companions, but it is not our reason for bicycling.

I now bicycle between four and five thousand miles each year, and a few years ago began bicycle commuting to work, which is an enjoyable twenty-five-mile round trip. I particularly like the early morning colors associated with the sunrise, and arrive at work alert and ready to get started. The ride home at the end of the day is relaxing both physically and mentally, and it also sharpens my appetite in a non-fattening way. At night I sleep soundly and in the morning awake refreshed. In summary, I bicycle because I enjoy it, but I also enjoy the benefits of bicycling.

B. Wally Pierson

After many years of cycling, including boyhood and adulthood, I find myself heading for age fifty-nine and liking cycling as well today as when I was a young man. To write this, I must tell you of my better half, Mary, who, after all these years still finds herself on the back of our own tandem, still pedaling along.

In the late thirties and early forties, we found ourselves riding with the South Shore Cycle Club. This was a very active club with short rides and weekend rides, all part of our courting. We found we were living in a world of cycling with most of our friends enjoying the same sport. Being a spectator at the Humbolt Park races was also part of the scene for the South Shore Club. We would ride from the south side of Chicago to the far west side to spend an evening viewing the races. I, too, tried my hand at racing, but shortly I knew that touring was the part of cycling for me.

Mary and I were married in June of 1940. Money as tight as it was, we started our married life on the seats of two bicycles, honeymooning through Wisconsin, a trip with lasting, happy memories, even thirty-seven years later. During these years all clubs were active and there was always somewhere to go. A ride to Michigan City or Cedar Lake were fine weekend adventures.

Our family started and we found ourselves riding our two sons, Bob and Don, on the homemade baby bicycle seats. Then World War II interrupted to break up our cycling for a few years.

Several years later with our last two children, cycling started all over again. In the early sixties, with the bike-boom starting, we found ourselves riding alone. The thrill of the bike came back and we were touring again with Tom, twelve, and Patty, seven. Many short summer trips were enjoyed by the family and before long, we were living again on the bikes.

Tom at this time started racing and this kept the whole family busy. During these years we were members of the West Suburban Wheelmen, with both father and son enjoying club racing. Tom and I had the pleasure of riding the last two Elgin-to-Chicago races together.

Our family enjoyment lived on as we followed racing, taking Tom as far as California to ride the Nationals in 1965, loving every minute of the excitement we all felt.

My wife wasn't riding too much during these years due to all the chasing of our racing son, but soon college came along and we found time once again to enjoy cycling with our daughter, Patty.

As the miles and years went by we thought about riding tandem. This proved a huge success and opened another, new world of the two-seater. A trip around Lake Michigan on a used tandem gave us the urge to buy a new custom-built tandem and we chose a Jack Taylor. Thus, the plans for a European trip were in the making.

In 1969, we decided to go to England and personally pick up our custom Taylor, this being one of the real highlights of our cycling experiences. A thirty-day trip through England and Ireland was a dream fulfilled for Mary, Pat and myself.

I have had the pleasure of riding centuries (100 miles) and double centuries (200 miles) and tours as famous as the Tour

*of the Scioto River Valley, back in the days of forty-two partici-
pants as compared with the thousands of today. Only a cyclist
knows the pleasure of riding a century with his thirteen-year-old
daughter and returning the next week to ride a double century
marathon.*

*Today, we are enjoying club rides with various clubs, in-
cluding our Palos Park Pedal Pushers, which I had the pleasure
of forming a few years back. We still put the bags on the bike
and enjoy a weekend overnighter. There is always somewhere
to go on our tandem and always someone new to get involved.
Recently, we helped a young couple get into the sport on an
old-fashioned farmland ride. After forty miles of pleasure through
the countryside they shared with us the feeling that, even with
the sore muscles, they'd never had so much fun—conveniently and
inexpensively.*

*In the last few years, I taught cycling at our local junior
college and had still another unusual experience. So many people,
young and old, are really anxious to discover the pleasures of
cycling and I'm lucky to know how to help them in that discovery.*

*Our future looks bright in cycling. We are anxiously looking
forward to many more years of enjoying this sport with all of the
wonderful friends we have made. At check-up time our doctor
simply nods and says "keep pedaling."*

*One thing about cycling not found in every sport is its
availability. There's always a road, always a new mile to seek
out. The choice is there—a thirty-day planned tour or a thirty-
mile spur-of-the-moment ride through the country. All you need
is your bike and your enthusiasm!*

*As a final thought, I am grateful to the sport of cycling for
the many, many friends and acquaintances Mary and I have
made. Over the years, we have maintained friendships with
young and old—for anyone who wants to can enjoy a bike.*

C. Lloyd W. Jones

*From short 7-mile tours on a three-speed to 850-mile, four-
teen-day tours on a lightweight ten-speed, I rediscovered bicycling
over the past ten years. After an absence from the bicycle for
almost thirty years I now find myself hanging around bicycle
shops discussing derailleurs, gear ratios, the relative merits of side*

6-11 & 6-12: Lloyd W. Jones—Bicycle "driver."

pull versus center pull brakes, high pressure, low profile clincher tires, and such things as examining the latest innovations in new bicycle equipment.

Rediscovering bicycling has led to thousands of miles of bike touring for me and my family which includes, at various times, all four of my sons. It has been exciting and challenging to be a part of a recreational activity that has grown phenomenally in the last few years.

My involvement began when a friend loaned me a three-speed bicycle so I could join him and a few others on a short Boeing Bicycle Club tour. In 1967 it was a major event to get together for tours of five to fifteen miles.

From that point my interest grew rapidly to 100-mile weekend tours and overnite campouts. The culmination was my first major 450-mile tour from Seattle to the League of American Wheelmen Convention in 1972 in Salem, Oregon. Included in this six-day tour were children nine years old and adults in their sixties using single-speed bicycles. At times they were perhaps a little slower due to the hilly terrain, but they did make it the entire way without problems.

Many adults who haven't driven a bicycle in many years feel intimidated by what appears to be heavy traffic on all the streets and roads. On the contrary, freeways have created excellent bicycle facilities on back and frontage roads in many areas. Books for the bicyclist have been written to assist in tour planning which identify local bicycle routes. In the Northwest we have two fine guides to bicycle touring, entitled Bicycling the Backroads of Puget Sound *and* Bicycling the Backroads of Northwest Washington, *both by Bill and Erin Woods. There is considerable reference material available on where and how to tour and commute by bicycle which can be found in local libraries, book stores, state and city transportation departments, park departments, and local bicycle clubs and organizations.*

The League of American Wheelmen (LAW), the oldest bicycling organization in America, founded in 1880, holds an annual "September Century Run" which I have participated in for many years. The only requirement is to be able to ride one hundred miles over a designated course in under twelve hours. To the novice this may seem like a formidable task, but a participant in this event soon discovers that it is not so difficult and is generally surprised at how easy it is to complete within the allotted time. In fact, for some first-time entrants, the ease of completing the recently instituted half-century (50 miles) usually encourages them to return the following year as century riders. Many centuries are drawing over five hundred entries each year.

My bicycling interest led me and five other people to organize the Northwest Bicycle Touring Society (NBTS) in 1974. Each year we provide six major tours of 100 to 850 miles which can extend for two to fourteen days and which are open to all bicyclists.

Each year these tours, which include trips around Mt. Rainier in the fall, the San Juan Islands, Century Runs, and longer tours into British Columbia and Canada, have been completely filled well before the starting dates. Although most of us could be self-sufficient for bicycle touring each tour is accompanied by a single vehicle or "sag wagon" which carries gear, some spare parts, and is equipped to handle emergencies. This is important when handling groups of up to 130 bicyclists. Eliminating the requirement that you have to carry all your own equipment opens the tours up to a greater cross-section of people, including families with younger children.

On longer tours of two-week duration, each day's cycling is limited to forty to sixty miles. Starting early in the day means finishing in plenty of time to enjoy each night's camp and associated recreational activities.

Once the initial cost outlay has been made for the bike, bicycling is extremely economical. However, it should be noted that as you become more serious you tend to become a little more sophisticated in your selection of gears, tires, brakes, etc.

The only fuel burned is calories. The ability to travel independently over long distances with a minimum of equipment on the most efficient vehicle ever designed is extremely rewarding. The sights and sounds experienced through the mobility of the bicycle are unique.

A properly maintained bicycle requires little preparation to "take a tour." In most instances all that is needed is to just get on and go, or perhaps carry the bicycle by auto a short distance to a starting point.

We bicycle because we love the freedom the bicycle gives us, the independence from burning of fossil fuels, the quietness of transportation, the friends and acquaintances we have made, the variety of experiences and the healthful exercise it affords.

Whether you prefer to bicycle alone, with a good friend, as a member of a bicycle club, or as a part of an organized tour, don't wait. Join me in an exhilarating eighteen-mile run down Mt. Rainier from Paradise, through Stevens Canyon to Ohanapecosh. You will soon forget the thirteen-mile ascent that was required that morning.

D. Larry Pichman

Cycling is not new with me. During my school summers, I delivered Western Union telegrams on my bike. I had my first new bike in 1934, for selling newspaper subscriptions. During World War II, I was in the Air Force and used the bike as a means of transportation around the post even though I had a staff car at my command.

At the close of World War II, my wife and I spent weekends riding our bikes. The following years, while building our home and having our family, bike riding was at a minimum. But a common interest always dominates in the long run. Neighbors of ours also biked for many years and soon our family joined and we rode together. In the early sixties, as members of the American Youth Hostel, we cycled with many people who, for years, were devoted cyclists, who contributed and inspired many a person to enjoy cycling.

To arise at 4:00 a.m., go to 5:00 a.m. church and start riding at 6:00 a.m. is one thing, but when half of our family was doing the same, it was something else. We completed our first half-century when our oldest child was sixteen years old and our youngest was eight. Even today, years later, they still talk about that ride. In 1963 we finished our first full century as a family.

The sport of cycling seemed to be a common interest and our family took advantage of it as a means of togetherness. My sales work had me out of town quite a bit, so when time permitted we would ride our bikes. It was a way to see things that were difficult to enjoy while in an automobile passing at higher speeds. It enabled us to enjoy conversation time while resting along the road, maybe under a shade tree, or in one of our heavy, rural old-time cemeteries, or just eating a snack that was brought along just for the occasion. What a delightful way to daydream.

For rides that were not close to where we live, I designed a roof bike carrier to hold six bikes. Today that may not impress people, but in the sixties, it brought conversation.

Then, in 1964, the World's Fair in New York pulled our family to the East Coast. We "hosteled" in Massachusetts, on Cape Cod and Nantucket. Our bikes enabled our family to enjoy each other and see our beautiful country.

The Palos Park Pedal Pushers was formed as a bike club, a family club with children from two to twenty-three. Our activities consisted of hosting cyclecrosses, group picnics, lunch and dinner rides, local rides, and overnight rides. Some rides began some three hundred miles away from home. As a bike club, we rode with many other bike groups and clubs such as those in Wheeling, Evanston, and Franklin.

1971—Four couples from our club went to Homestead, Florida, to ride with the Dr. Paul Dudley White Bike Club and then went to Grand Island in the Bahamas as their guests.

1972—Three couples from our club joined a tour group. By June, 1973, after nine months of planning, we were on our way to Zurich, Switzerland. Our trip took us through Switzerland, France, Germany, Luxembourg and Belgium. Then, via boat, we crossed the English Channel to Dover, England. Then, eight wonderful days to London. The entire trip was thirty-five days of beautiful weather, scenery, companionship, meeting new friends and customs—all of this made possible by means of the bicycle and good friendship.

Bike trips and conventions have taken us from the East Coast to the West Coast. Regardless of the ride, the season, or the place, as long as everybody comes with a bike, you can be sure you will enjoy yourself.

The more serious side of bike riding is the continuous need for recognition on the road and the everlasting pleas to make cycling a safer and more enjoyable sport for every member of the family.

Some of the projects I have undertaken in the past have been to give talks on safety to Boy Scouts, Brownies and Girl Scouts; help plan, direct and lay out a course for marathons, century rides, and cyclecross; give a course in bicycle maintenance; show slides of our bike rides to other groups; work with planning committees; and serve two terms as president of our bike club.

The benefits that can be derived from cycling are many. It mostly depends on you, what you might want to achieve and how hard you try. As a beginner, it is great to say how far you rode. As you improve in riding, the satisfaction you gain will be that much greater. Regardless of the type of ride or how hard it seemed at the end of the ride, the tired feeling will leave you completely filled with a sense of accomplishment.

Cycling is a vehicle for friends to relive experiences with. It is not to brag about, but it is something to tell stories about. The anticipation and planning involved in being part of someone else's programs are rewarding.

The New Years I Cycle bicycle ride is a lakefront ride. January 1 seems to be the warmest night at the coldest time, as we bring in a new year and remember the things that we didn't do last year.

E. Harriett E. Milbourn

My husband and I started biking thirteen years ago in our forty-ninth year and hope never to have to give it up. Our adventurous investment in ten-speed bikes was brought about by the frustrating experience of working in windowless offices, and converted warehouses; we became desperate in our desire and need for outdoor exercise. Desire for an activity which both of us could enjoy, either alone or together, plus the proximity of a good bicycle shop, led to the decision to ride bicycles.

Fortunately, the dealer who sold us our first bikes strongly recommended ten-speeds. Even though we felt self-conscious learning to ride them—adults riding bikes at that time (1965) were oddities—we are grateful for his advice. To get started we rode them after dark on the street-lighted sidewalk until we mastered the gears and hand brakes, the toe clips and the underslung handlebars. In retrospect, we are sure that, had we settled for single- or three-speed vehicles, we would not be riding today— too much energy is needed for the exercise involved.

The first year we participated in the Great Eastern Rally (now known as GEAR) held in Bowmansville, Pennsylvania, and from then on we were really hooked. Being campers, we found biking and camping mixed very conveniently. That July we put the two bikes and all our camping gear into the Volkswagen "bug" and headed for the Fingerlake Region of New York State. There we cycled around Owasco (thirty-five miles), Skaneateles (forty-two miles), Canandaigua (fifty miles), Keuka (fifty miles) and Seneca (eighty-five miles); one lake a day with one day's rest in between, except the first two which we did on consecutive days.

In the fall, we bought a fifteen-speed tandem and when Thanksgiving Day was approaching, we thought it just might be an ideal day to try it on the open road. We planned a cookout and were not disappointed because the day dawned bright and beautiful. We packed our knapsack with spareribs, yams, red cabbage relish, homemade cookies, a thermos of V8 and another thermos of hot coffee, strapped it on the back of the tandem and pedaled to a suburban park. Have you ever eaten spareribs cooked over an open fire, or yams wrapped in foil and baked in hot coals? DELICIOUS! And the accompanying odors are as savory as the Thanksgiving turkey roasting. After that we wondered why we hadn't taken up biking sooner and recommended to all our relatives and friends that if any felt the need for a new lease on life—try cycling.

For the next eight years we spent our vacations and holidays attending various bike get-togethers from the East Coast to as far West as Wisconsin and as far South as New Orleans and Homestead, Florida. Also during that time we were active members of bike clubs and found them stimulating and rewarding.

Since our retirement in 1972 when we moved to Florida, we find riding along with a few friends the better way. In analyzing this feeling we've decided that by setting our own pace, it is more relaxing. We do try to get to one bike rally each year so we can keep in touch with our former biking friends and meet new enthusiasts.

The DeLand, Florida, area is a perfect place for bicycling. There are numerous streets where there is little auto traffic and what there is moves slowly. The county roads surrounding the town are hard-surfaced; many are tree-lined and have very little traffic. On these roads we ride through beautiful horse country, farmlands and groves of oranges, grapefruit and tangerines. In orange blossom season, nothing can surpass the soothing experience of the fragrance sifting through your nostrils.

We ride every day. Because we are both retired, we don't have to plan for it, we just go whenever we want to. I try not to stay off my bike for more than one day. It makes us feel so great that it is easy to stick to it. In fact, if we don't get on our

6-13: During a tour from Pensacola to Panama City with six other couples (1968).

6-14: The first ride, Philadelphia, Pennsylvania (1965).

6-15: The Milbourns (center) preparing for a tour with friends.

bikes we feel like something is missing. When we miss, it is more difficult to cope. Biking gives us a feeling of well-being like nothing else can. It makes us feel so versatile.

My reason for riding is that it gives me a genuine feeling of well-being. If I'm happy and content, a bike ride emphasizes the feeling; if I'm disturbed or upset a bike ride releases the tension and clears my mind. Since I don't drive a car, I can go all about town on my bike, which gives me a feeling of independence. Presently, we lawn bowl regularly and I swim a half-mile each day. However, my first love is riding my bike.

Another thing I should like to relate is that the year before we started riding bikes I had a real problem with my joints swelling which the doctor diagnosed as arthritis. The winter after I took up riding I was no longer affected. Naturally I feel that the exercise stimulated circulation and hence no more swelling. Really my only health problem now is high cholesterol and I shudder to think of the condition I would be in today had I not started biking when I did!

I'm an advocate of biking regularly and am convinced that it's a marvelous "way to play."

6-16: Bicycle track racing is becoming more and more popular. Here the Kaiser family rides for fun at the Trexlertown Velodrome in Pennsylvania.

As the preceding examples have shown, the bicycle is more than a means to recreation; it is a way to experience the rich, human texture of life. In the words of California Bike Shop owner Ted Ernst, Jr., the "bicycle provides a oneness, a closeness, a communion with the world around you. It gets to be a philosophy, a way of life."

To participate in this "way of life" is a simple matter. If you don't have a bicycle, ask a cycling friend for suggestions about what kind of equipment to buy. Visit your local bike shop and ask for advice.

If you are interested in touring or in helping to discover and mark trails in your community, join your local bicycle club. Write to the League of American Wheelmen, 19 South Bothwell, Palatine, Illinois 60067. Write to the International Bicycle Touring Society, 846 Prospect St., LaJolla, California 92037, which arranges bicycle tours in various parts of the world. Write to Bikecentennial, P.O. Box 5308, Missoula, Montana 59807, which is developing bicycle trails in America. Join American Youth Hostels, Inc. National Campus, Delaplane, Virginia 22025 to receive a pass that enables you to lodge during a bicycle tour (or other outdoor trip) at any of the 150 youth hostels in the country (and the many overseas). If you want to learn how you can "discover" bikeways in your community, write for the *Planning for Bikeways* pamphlet and information: Bureau of Outdoor Recreation, Southeast Regional Office, 148 International Boulevard, Atlanta, Georgia 30303. If you are interested in road or track (velodrome) racing, contact the United States Cycling Federation, P.O. Box 699, Wall Street Station, New York, N.Y. 10005.

And by all means, ride.

chapter 7

The Chase

by Caroline Ringo

Perhaps the ultimate play activity could be considered one which can be conducted within a social setting requiring little equipment and involving family and friends.

Is there such an activity? According to a growing legion of enthusiasts throughout the country, the sport of orienteering would meet all the above requirements.

Orienteering is the art of navigating through an unknown area using a map and a compass as guides. It can be done for sport or it can be done for pleasure with no goal beyond that of a pleasant family outing with a stop for a picnic by some scenic spot.

According to Bob and Janet Putnam (and daughter, Kate), "The attraction of the sport is on two levels for us. The first is the 'competitive' aspect, which feels very much like you've always imagined a treasure hunt would feel. Secondly, we appreciate the sheer joy of seeing some of the most beautiful forests. The time spent in the woods during the spring, with the blooming flowers, and during the fall, with the colors and crisp leaves, is reward enough.

"There's never any great distance to travel to any meet, no physical size or strength requirements, and the whole course can be traveled at the speed you choose. There's no direct pressure to perform in such a sport since you are not competing directly with anybody. There's rarely an audience to upset those who are reluctant to participate.

"We enjoy the excitement of participatory sport that lasts longer than most sports events yet involves nothing more than

7-1: Putnam examines master map while daughter Kate looks on.

7-2: Janet Putnam leads the way while husband Bob gives Kate a vantage point for spotting red and white markers.

moving your feet and exercising your native instincts for the woods. Very few opportunities exist today to test your instincts in a completely natural environment without elaborate paraphernalia. Orienteering makes use of a compass but, after all, it's one of the oldest, lightest and simplest of tools.

"Philosophically, we both agree with the idea that people's ability to deal with the world at large and their own peace of mind are enhanced by successfully dealing with the natural environment on a personal basis. Orienteering offers such a test and also a change from worldly competition with all the material risks. In concentrating on the object of the game and the elements of the setting, we have found true recreation. To have achieved some proficiency in outdoor living taps a well of pride which holds, among other things, the pioneer spirit, a healthy bit of anarchy, and good old Yankee self-sufficiency.

"The do-it-yourself competition helps our family renew a natural association with the simpler things and brings with it a refreshing peace of mind. Any adventure a family can join in together which teaches respect for the freer things in the world and offers a respite from pressures and anxieties is an ideal way to revitalize energies.

"Having a three-year-old daughter to take along is a particular bonus. A child's world today is so dominated by the technological aspects of modern living, and especially by the non-participatory recreation of television, that we believe it more vital than ever to provide a balance to these influences. Part of the balance consists of instilling an easy facility with outdoor living. Without overdoing the wilderness survival thing, we hope to leave Kate with a deep appreciation of all aspects of outdoor enjoyment, from overnight camping to searching for fungi to just not getting lost.

"The real point of the sport is to participate in a game primarily with yourself on a court which is unequaled for diversity or accessibility."

A Sport for All Ages

As the Putnams have so eloquently stated, orienteering is well suited for all ages. Year-old children have completed the course sleeping soundly in carriers on their parents' backs. Parents have proudly proclaimed as they handed in their control cards: "Our two-year-old walked all the way."

For children, spotting the red and white markers in the woods equals the excitement of an Easter egg hunt and makes orienteering more interesting for them than regular hiking. It is not unusual for children, bursting with energy, to race ahead of their parents to the finish line waving the control card. Earlier, the same parents had wondered whether the children could ever complete the course.

According to the Delaware Valley Orienteering Association, the usual pattern for family orienteering is for the family to participate as one group for the first few meets until they are familiar with map reading and compass work. Then friendly "differences of opinion" might arise concerning the choice of routes between points. After all, this is why orienteering is nicknamed the "thinking man's sport." At finish line post-mortems, over cups of hot chocolate or coffee, you hear comments like: "I told ya, Dad, if we'd followed the trail to the bend then cut across the field, instead of taking a bearing through the woods and getting lost in the sticker bushes. . ."

At the next meet, the group might split up for some friendly rivalry, with Mom and Sis trying to complete the course in a shorter time than Dad and Junior. Eventually, as orienteering skills grow, the kids will challenge the grownups—and often win!

Senior citizens go orienteering—not at the same pace as the young student representing his college orienteering club, of course, but at a pace comfortable for them. In fact, orienteering, because it involves leisurely walking with companions in a tranquil natural setting, is ideal for senior citizens. Bob Walk of Levittown, Pennsylvania, became interested in orienteering in his early fifties after suffering two heart attacks. He reports that, "I compete in the over-45 class and find that I place well up among the better elapsed times for any given meet. So age and physical condition are not necessarily a drawback to following orienteering. For that reason I would recommend the sport enthusiastically to individuals and families as one of the few inexpensive and rewarding activities left to us."

In Sweden, orienteering is a complete sport; it is a form of recreation that can be practiced for a lifetime. In that country, it is not uncommon for someone to begin orienteering at age seven and stay with the sport for more than half a century. So, like run-

7-3: Bob Walk, veteran orienteer, demonstrates use of map and compass to newcomers.

ning and cycling, orienteering can be practiced at any age. It can be a non-competitive lifesport.

In this country, non-competitive orienteers often participate in twosomes. Winning times need not be important to the orienteer. Everyone can win at orienteering if he selects the goal right for him. Perhaps you want a quiet stroll to observe and photograph the birds and wildflowers. If so, orienteering is the answer. Or perhaps your goal is to locate all of the markers on the course, regardless of the time it takes you.

Equipment

Orienteering requires little equipment. You will likely have appropriate clothes and shoes in your wardrobe for this sport. Long pants are recommended if there are sticker bushes on the course. Wide, flared pant legs can slow you down when you're running, especially if they're wet from rain or if you've decided the quickest route is wading through the stream instead of crossing the bridge. Jeans are ideal for orienteering and so are sneakers, unless you expect to do a lot of climbing over rocks, in which case you might want the firmer support of a hiking shoe. Jackets that will not catch on bushes are best. Nylon windbreakers are ideal and can be tied around your waist if you get too warm. Days that seem cold and windy at the starting point often seem much more pleasant once you are in the woods and exercising. Most meets place no restrictions on the color of clothing worn, though at major meets, where competition is keen, all red clothing is usually banned to avoid competitors being mistaken at a distance for markers.

Part of the small registration fee for an orienteering meet provides each individual or group with a detailed contour map of the area where the meet is being held. Some orienteers like to carry this in a transparent map case hung by a cord around their necks. For ski or bicycle orienteering, this frees the hands, but many foot orienteers prefer to carry the map, turning it so the direction of travel is always at the top of the map and keeping a thumb on their approximate location at all times. If you don't have a map case, you should have a plastic bag to protect the map in case of rain.

7-4: Maps, time cards, and instructions can be found at the registration table before every orienteering meet.

7-5: Meet officials Kent and Caroline Ringo keeping a record of participants' time cards.

One of my most frightening moments in orienteering was finding myself caught in a sudden downpour a couple of miles from the starting point. I knew where I was when the rain started, but in minutes, the map was a soggy mass and the dark sky meant there was not much daylight left. Fortunately, another orienteer came along and allowed me to look at his map, but I learned at least two things from that experience: 1) always have a plastic sandwich bag in your pocket in case of rain, and 2) get in the habit of studying the map enough to memorize the general direction of roads and streams bounding the area, plus major trails, clearings or landmarks such as a firetower or high hill, and their relationship to the starting point.

If the meet is one in which you don't receive the map for your course until after your starting signal has been given, there is usually a map posted at the starting area which you can study before you start the course. Decide in advance what to do if you become lost. On which side of the course are the main roads? the swamps?

Your compass is probably your most important piece of equipment and I suggest that you carry one along even though you will sometimes be able to complete your course by map-reading only. Any compass will tell which way is north and give you the bearing to any given point, but the easiest to use is the protractor base type such as those marketed by the Silva Company. This type allows you to rotate the compass housing with respect to the base in which it is mounted.

There are three easy steps in using it. First, lay the compass on the map with the edge of the base parallel to your direction of travel, being sure the arrow on the base of the compass points in the direction in which you want to go. Second, while holding the base in this position, rotate the compass housing until the grid lines which represent north on the map lie directly under the grid lines on your compass. Third, pick up the compass and hold it horizontal in front of you. Rotate your body until the compass needle swings around and is superimposed over the needle painted on the compass base. You have now locked your bearing into your compass. Standing directly behind the compass, notice where the direction of travel arrow is pointing. Pick out a tree, bush, or other landmark in the distance, walk to it, pick out another distant landmark in your path and continue as long as you want to keep that same bearing.

There are many models of orienteering compasses available. One of the least expensive is available at Boy Scout supply counters. You can usually rent a compass at meets until you are ready to buy your own. If you purchase a compass, I recommend a liquid damped compass because the needle will settle faster, and the time you save by not having to wait for the needle to swing back and forth makes the extra investment worthwhile. Most compasses have a ruler along one edge of the rectangular base. This is useful in measuring distances on the map so that you can convert distance into paces or yards or meters according to the scale of the map you are using. Some of the expensive models come with a set of snap-on edges which you interchange according to the scale of the map you are using and give readings directly in that scale. Another feature which some orienteers appreciate is a clicker attachment on the compass which helps them keep track of the number of paces they have covered.

The First Meet

So much for equipment. We'll assume that you've arrived at your first orienteering meet and are wondering what to expect. Look for the registration table where you will be asked to sign your name and address and the names of the people in your party. You will receive a map and a control card. Some meets have maps pre-marked for each course. At others, you are given a contour map onto which you must copy the points from a master map, either before or after the timekeeper has given you a starting time. The location of each control point is indicated by a circle of about ¼-inch in diameter. Each circle is numbered in the same order as that in which you are expected to locate the markers and a line is drawn connecting the circles so that the general length and shape of the course are readily apparent. There will probably be a list of clues which you should copy, such as "the depression," or "the clearing, southwest corner" which will help you to locate the markers. The approximate length of the course will also be given.

Courses range in length and difficulty from a very short white one which is the beginner's or wayfarer's course through yellow, orange, red and finally blue, which is the elite course for experienced competitive orienteers in top physical condition. The color

7-6: David Brown, a member of the Delaware Valley Orienteering Association (Penna.), carefully copies control point locations from the master map.

names are used for convenience only. The markers you will be looking for will all be the standard diagonally striped red and white ones, regardless of which course you are on. (International rules have recently authorized use of orange rather than red so that color-blind individuals will not be at a disadvantage in competition, so you may possibly be finding markers that are orange and white instead of red and white if your club has already converted.) Most meets will have two or more courses to choose from and the people at the registration desk will be glad to help you select the one best for you.

After you are sure that you understand how to use the compass, look at the map to see if you know the meaning of the symbols and lines. Contour lines indicate elevation above sea level. You will soon learn to recognize hills, valleys, streams and some orienteering terms like "re-entrant" (an elongated sloping valley) and "saddle" (a low point on a ridge connecting two summits). The scale of the map will also be given. This is useful in keeping track of how far it is between points. If you've taken the time before the meet to mark off a measured distance and walk from one end to the other, counting your double paces as you walk in your usual hiking stride, some simple arithmetic will give you the length of your usual stride and you can tell approximately how many paces you will take between points. Ordinarily, map scales used in orienteering are between 1:10,000 and 1:20,000, which means that one inch on the map equals 10,000 inches on the ground. Many clubs use United States Geological Survey maps which are available in a scale of 1:24,000. A free index for each state gives the name and location of each quadrangle and you can then order specific maps for $1.25 each. The address is The U.S. Geological Survey, 1200 South Eads Street, Arlington, Virginia 22202

On your map there will also be symbols representing such things as buildings, quarries, swamps, and cemeteries, and lines representing streams, intermittent streams, power lines, railroads, trails, primitive roads, highways, etc. Be sure you understand all of these before going into the woods. A key to these symbols is available at no charge when you order the geological survey maps. Due to the high cost involved in making the four or five color maps used at national meets, most maps you will encounter will probably be black and white photocopies. The color maps can show clearings, kinds of ground cover and many other useful details not as readily recognizable in black and white. Don't give up on orienteering until you've given it a fair chance with a really good map.

If you are practicing orienteering skills on your own instead of at a meet, the USGS maps referred to are probably what you will be using. They are in color and are easy to read, but they may be several years out of date. You must be constantly aware that trails may have become overgrown, that buildings might have been constructed or torn down, and roads added or relocated since the map was printed. A good orienteering map is field checked just before a meet to insure accuracy. Sometimes symbols are added for features such as large boulders, cliffs, hunters' stands, and other features useful to the course-setter and the orienteer.

Before you start the course be sure to note the time at which markers will be taken in. Respect this for your own safety, if for no other reason. In the late autumn darkness comes early and the course-setters want to be sure that everyone is out of the woods. Also, they may have to remove the control markers on the day of the meet and will appreciate as much daylight as possible. If you ever set a course and have to explain to a park ranger what you're doing out there in the woods with a lantern when the sign clearly says the park closes at sundown, you'll know what I mean.

OK, are you ready to start? Do you have your map, compass, plastic bag (in case of rain, remember), and whistle, plus canteen, candy bar or whatever you want in the way of nourishment. Competitive orienteers travel light, but nobody will laugh if you start out with a picnic basket, camera and binoculars. Just remember not to leave any litter behind you. Orienteers have a good record for respecting the natural environment.

Assuming that you have double-checked your map against the master to be absolutely sure that you copied all the points in exactly the right location, you are now ready to check in with the timekeeper. He or she will be sure that both parts of your control card are properly filled out, giving your name, course and class. The class symbols are a way of separating contestants into categories based on sex, age or degree of orienteering experience. These classifications vary from club to club and may be fairly general such as YF (young female under age eighteen), GC (a group with at least one child age ten or under) or OM (older male age forty-three or over). In national meets the nomenclature used is H and D for the German "Herren" and "Damen," and the age brackets are much more precise. The classification D15-18 A would mean an event for girls aged fifteen to eighteen who have chosen to run the A or more difficult level of competition. This system enables you to compare your time with that of others on the same course who competed in the same class, even though many others in other classes may have also run the same course. Thus your time may have been only the tenth fastest on the yellow course, but only one other contestant in your class may have had a faster time than you did.

The timekeeper will keep the stub of your card for his records and to post on the bulletin board when you return. This board shows the standing of each competitor as he finishes. Some clubs do not post results at the meet, preferring to mail results to those who participated. Since starting times are staggered over a couple of hours, not everyone wants to wait around until the last contestant has finished in order to find out who had the fastest time.

The main part of your control card is carried with you on the course. Some orienteers keep it in a pocket while others prefer to place it inside the map case where it won't get lost, punching through case, map and control. If you lose your control card, continue the course, punching the rest of the symbols on the map itself. There is always a chance that another orienteer will find your card and turn it in so that you will receive full credit. Be sure to report a lost card to the timekeeper so he will know you are back. At each control point you will find a red and white or orange and white cloth marker with a punch hanging from it. Since the symbol of each punch is different, they furnish proof of how many controls you visited.

We will assume that you are on a white course, which is the one usually selected by beginning orienteers. Markers on this course should be fairly easy to find. They will usually be at or near a trail intersection, at a bend in a stream, beside a building, on top of a hill, etc. If you don't find the marker, it probably means that you didn't read your map correctly or that you failed to count paces and may be at the wrong trail intersection, hilltop, etc. As you successfully locate a few markers and your confidence grows, resist the impulse of assuming, when a marker isn't where you expect it to be, that either: 1) the course-setter made a mistake in placing the marker, or 2) someone carried off the marker before you found it. Neither is likely, although both have happened on occasion.

Several years ago at a meet at Valley Forge State Park, a park very popular with the public on Sunday afternoons, an orienteer found one of the markers lying on the ground. Probably it had been carried awhile, then dropped when a child tired of playing with it. In trying to help, the orienteer hung the marker where he thought it should go. This turned out not to be the correct location, which led to much confusion for the rest of the afternoon.

Markers occasionally disappear entirely during a meet despite attached tags which explain their purpose and request that they not be disturbed, and even more rarely a marker from a previous meet is accidentally left in the woods. This once happened at French Creek State Park when the course-setter for the Delaware Valley Orienteering Association placed a marker about thirty feet from one left in the woods the month before by the Drexel University Orienteering Club. He was not expecting another marker, so did not notice it. The timekeeper resolved the confusion by giving credit for finding either marker.

There will be few route choices on a white course, since al-

7-7: Hugh MacMullan copying clues before starting course.

most all of it will be on trails. On other courses there will be at least two logical ways of going from one control to the next. Let me emphasize that there is no one right route choice, and this is why orienteering is referred to as "cunning running." If your cross-country navigation is not too accurate but you are the star of the school cross-country team, you would probably prefer to choose a longer route using trails. If you are not a good runner but are able to accurately follow contours and compass bearings, you would most likely choose a more direct route through the woods.

The following first-person account by Hugh MacMullan and his four children, aged four to twelve at the time of the meet, vividly takes you into the sport of orienteering as a family activity.

The Chase

"Based on what we had been able to learn, orienteering appeared to offer exactly what we needed. It was to be outside, in the woods, quiet, would require some physical effort as well as mental concentration, the cost appeared nominal, and most important, we could do it together. It sounded like the ultimate in family participatory sports.

"We arrived at the starting area and signed up for a try at the yellow course. A longer red course (about five miles) and an easier white course were also available. Registration costs were $.25 for each of the kids and $.50 for me, plus $.25 for a compass rental. We decided to rent two, so that total costs were $2. We received a contour map, enthusiastic instructions on orienteering map and compass work for beginners, a starting time, and wishes for good luck from the course-setter. After we copied the check points onto our map from a master map, we began orienteering in earnest, excitedly walking off down a pine needle-carpeted trail leading to the first of five markers.

"The first control was located on our map near the intersection of a small path and our trail. As with all properly set courses, there were at least two routes to the marker. We could continue on the trail we were on for the entire route, marking off intersecting trails and doing some pacing until we were to the correct intersection. This approach seemed the best, but was certainly the longest as the trail meandered before it hit the desired path. An-

7-8: Map and compass in hand, Huey MacMullan decides
upon his choice of routes.

other approach was to take a compass shot through the woods,
'aiming off' to the right of the path/trail intersection and using the
well-marked trail as a collecting feature. This approach would
certainly be the fastest if we made no mistakes.

"We settled quickly on the slow but sure approach, saving
any daring maneuvers for later in the course. Our pacing and trail
counting led us after twenty minutes or so to what we believed
was the correct intersection. A compass bearing proved this to be
accurate, and we proudly came upon our first red and white
marker hanging from a tree branch, seen first by a very excited
Huey. Lauren punched the control card in the box marked 1; and
we moved away from the marker and considered our approach to
the next control.

"The next marker appeared to be located on the west side of
an earthen cranberry bog dike. A dirt road crossed the dike to the
east and ran down the east side to the south. We were located on
the southwest side of the bog, giving us the options of taking the
long way around and across on the road, or the short way up the
west side of the bog, through a marshy area. We sent Huey fifty
feet or so into the marsh to check conditions. He came back
quickly, with one sneaker muddy to the ankle, and reported that
it 'looked OK to him.' We considered his muddy ankle more
significant than his 'OK,' and started off the long, dry way.

"Ann had to be carried on my shoulders for a short spell towards the end of the leg, and we let her punch the control card
from 'the saddle' when we found it. It was very close to where we
thought it would be; and we were becoming increasingly pleased
with ourselves.

"The next control's clue said simply, 're-entrant'; and the map
and its contour lines showed it to be located in a kind of small
dead-end valley in the side of a hill, next to two similar features.
The route choices offered included a direct approach that would
take us up and down all the contour lines, another approach that
took us near the top of the hill via a trail, and a third approach
ending near the bottom of the hill via a path and dry stream bed.

"Since I was going to have to carry Ann, I vetoed the direct
approach up and down the hills. We decided that we could more
readily recognize a re-entrant from its mouth near the bottom of
the hill and so took the low road. We made our first mistake on
this control, and went up the wrong re-entrant. Amy eventually

7-9: Huey MacMullan takes a bearing and heads across the field toward his next attack point.

got us straightened out by running back and properly counting re-entrants from the stream bed, after which we found the marker with little trouble.

"We saved our only daring maneuver for the last marker. According to the map, it was located dead in the center of a triangular-shaped wooded area, bounded by a hard-surface road, a well-worn trail, and a small path. The surest way to the control was very roundabout. It would have been to hike the small path to the trail, pace the trail to an abandoned gravel pit (marked on the map with crossed picks), from there take a compass shot to a dry stream bed, follow the stream bed to its end, and finally take another short compass bearing to the marker. On the other hand, we could take one long, adventurous compass shot from the junction of the small path and road. If we missed the marker, we'd probably go right on past, all the way to the trail. Nevertheless, flushed with success, this way was our unanimous choice.

"As we moved into the woods, Lauren became our steady aiming point. We moved her around left or right some fifty or sixty feet ahead of us until she lined up with the compass bearing, then we'd pace up to her, counting as we went, and begin again. Huey and Amy paced, I worked one compass, and Ann tagged along behind. Soon the woods got thicker, Amy and Huey began openly disagreeing on how far we'd gone, Ann wanted to be carried, and I was fighting a tendency to overrule my compass by moving Lauren slightly to the right on each shot.

"By the time we reached the approximate locale of the marker, Amy stopped, while Huey plowed on about two hundred feet further. I struck a compromise between them, called them all in and began sending out search missions fifty paces in each direction. My faithful scouts reported that the woods looked very much the same in all directions, with nary a sign of red or white.

"I then decided to calculate how far to the left the marker would be if my compass had been correct all along, rather than my sense of direction. Seventy paces in that direction brought us to a beautiful sight—the last marker. Now we ran in earnest, full of energy and sure of our direction back to the start/finish.

"We finished the course, pleased with ourselves and very excited about orienteering. We hung around the timekeeper for awhile, discussing our route selections and the day's courses, and orienteering in general with other friendly and enthusiastic people. We knew we were hooked on the sport there and then, and promised ourselves we'd be back again and again."

Starting from Scratch

Hugh MacMullan acknowledges that his family and he became "hooked on the sport there and then, and promised ourselves we'd be back again and again."

And what if you share this kind of enthusiasm? How do you get started? Let us assume that you would like to try orienteering and have written to the United States Orienteering Federation but they have no club listed in your area. Be sure to contact both the ROTC and the physical education departments of colleges within easy driving distance to see if they might have a club not yet affiliated with the USOF. Also contact hiking clubs, which are usually aware of other outdoor recreational organizations in the area.

What if all this fails and you cannot locate a club? The solution is to interest some more people and start a club of your own. However, before you organize a group of your own, by all means try to attend at least one meet of another club even if it means a rather lengthy trip. Also, you should be reading a few of the excellent books which have appeared recently on orienteering. Along with much valuable advice on setting a safe course the books give directions for making your own markers. You can make them from cloth and coat hanger wire, or you can improvise from other materials. One of the easiest is empty white plastic gallon milk jugs with the lids left on. Paint a diagonal red stripe on each side, mark each jug with a different letter or symbol and attach a string or wire for hanging. These are waterproof and will save you the expense of a set of punches. Each contestant will need to carry a pencil to use in copying the symbol onto the proper square on his control card, or you can hang a pencil at each marker.

Finding a suitable location for orienteering is the next step, since the area must be large enough for your purposes and you must be able to obtain permission from the landowner. County and state parks are logical choices, but you should also investigate state game lands and wildlife management areas. Public utility

7-10: Rain does not deter orienteers.

companies, lumbering and mining companies may have suitable land which they will allow you to use. Terrain which offers a variety of contours is preferable, though relatively flat land can be used if it has enough trails, streams and other recognizable features to serve as attack points. Lebanon Forest in the New Jersey Pine Barrens is flat, but the Delaware Valley Orienteering Club has been orienteering there very successfully for several years.

In planning an orienteering event enlist as much help as you can. Movies about orienteering are available for free loan and could be shown at hiking clubs, community service clubs, school groups such as PTA, etc. Contact the Girl Scouts and Boy Scouts who have orienteering badges and may already have someone trained in orienteering. Don't turn down any offers of help, since you will eventually need people for registration, timekeeping, licking stamps and typing (if you mail out schedules or results), writing news releases, and many other jobs besides map revision and course-setting.

It is not my intention to go into the fine points of course-setting here. Some people, myself included, find it even more fun and challenge than competing, but it is a responsibility which should not be taken lightly. You wouldn't want to set a course in which the direct line from one marker to another was over a cliff, even if you expected everyone to be sensible enough to take the roundabout trail. Without really looking at the map some over-zealous competitor might take off headed straight for disaster. You'll probably feel better qualified for course-setting after you've gained some experience by participating at a few meets first. It is even better if you can volunteer to assist an experienced course-setter before you try a course of your own.

There are many variations of orienteering which can be done even in a limited space. Compass exercises and games suitable for use with young people are included in several of the orienteering books and offer a good introduction to the sport. Score orienteering is a popular variation from the cross-country or point-to-point type of meet that we have been describing. In score orienteering a large number of controls, each worth a given number of points according to its difficulty, are placed in the woods. More controls are used than could possibly be visited by any one contestant in the time allotted. A time limit is set and everyone starts at once. Controls can be visited in any order and it is up to each contestant to determine the best use of his allotted time, depending on his skill and endurance. Points are deducted for every minute a contestant exceeds the time limit. This is a good kind of meet for sharpening navigational skills and because of the mass start can be used on shorter fall days when you want to get everyone out of the woods before dark.

Orienteering also lends itself to relays, and such team events are included in many major meets. A popular form is the clover-leaf, in which each runner completes one leaf of the course and returns to the starting point so that the next teammate can start. Usually after a certain period of time the next runner is permitted to start even if the previous runner has not returned, thus keeping competition alive even after a poor start. This is a good form of orienteering for families or groups of mixed abilities.

A TRIM orienteering course is similar to score orienteering except that it lacks the time limit. A large number of markers are set in the woods where they can be left over a period of months. The course is publicized and maps are distributed showing the location of all markers. This is good for introducing beginners to the sport and also has numerous possibilities for improving skills and endurance of veteran orienteers. Since the markers are permanent, the course can be used at any time without supervision.

Ski orienteering is very popular in northern countries. It received Olympic status in 1949 although it has not yet been included in the Games. Other variations of orienteering include the use of snowshoes, bicycles, horses and canoes.

However, the most popular kind of orienteering is on land, in lush, natural settings, which can be found in or near most communities in this country. As more and more people are discovering, orienteering is one of the best ways to play.

To learn more about this exciting sport, contact the United States Orienteering Federation. Members receive a monthly newsletter, *The Control Point,* which lists future events and provides tips on how to improve orienteering skills. The federation also publishes a quarterly journal called *Orienteering—USA.*

Membership applications, an address list of clubs, an orienteering bibliography, and other information can be obtained by writing the United States Orienteering Federation, P.O. Box 500, Athens, Ohio 45701.

Information on orienteering compasses, books, films and equipment is available by writing The Silva Company, 2466 N. State Road 39, LaPorte, Indiana 46350.

chapter 8
The Dance

by Esther Frankel

You belong. You belong to a family, a community, a city, a country, the world. Yet can you think of a recreational activity that would allow you to walk over to two strangers anywhere, even in a foreign country, join hands with them, and become a part of a circle of other strangers, without knowing the language, or in fact, anyone in the group? Folk dance is just such a unique activity because it transcends geographic and language barriers. Perhaps man's primeval response to music and his basic need to communicate with his fellowman explains the universality of folk dance, for there is no place on earth where people do not dance. To share with others the joy of communal movement is to reinforce a feeling of belonging—to cement the unity of a community. You can't be lonely when you're folk dancing. Add to this departure from separateness the physical glow that comes from exercise, and you have the ideal form of play.

It has been said that man works for maintenance and plays for sustenance. People who don't take time out to play often suffer from excessive fatigue, even if the work they are doing does not involve physical effort. Play doesn't necessarily mean a mindless activity to kill time. It can be a time to learn, to grow as a human being. Folk dancing affords the individual the opportunity to learn about other people who share this ever-shrinking planet with us. In addition, its other attributes can be summed up in the credo of Ted Shawn, the father of American dance, "I believe that dance has the power to heal mentally and physically."

Interestingly, the word "mesmerize" comes from Franz Mesmer, an eighteenth-century physician who used collective dance to cure people's ailments. By interacting with others, on a non-verbal basis, even the shy lose their self-consciousness and gain a sense of perspective about their relationship with others in a group.

Mention the words "folk dance" to many Americans and they conjure up an image of eight people in a square do-si-do-ing and swinging partners to the accompaniment of a foot-stompin' fiddler and the twanged rhymes of a caller. Square dance is just one form of folk dance, but folk dance is not necessarily square dance.

What, then, is folk dance? As the name implies, folk dance is the expression of a people in organized movement. It reflects the temperament, environment, topography, climate, and the historical forces that shaped the character of the various societies. It is truly democratic because the dances were composed by the people, for the people, and performed by the people. These dances have been passed down from generation to generation, and like a coral chain, connect us to those who have gone before us and to those who will come after us. As such, folk dance can be called the heartbeat of all people, a mirror image of man. History can try to tell us about past eras and civilizations, but all too often the end result is a deplorable recounting of victories and defeats in war as recorded by the victors. Voltaire defined history as "a pack of lies told by the living about the dead." But the dance reflects the real lives of flesh and blood people like ourselves. Even the twentieth-century sophisticate can identify with the peasant who lived long before us because folk dance is a celebration of life. We may have acquired a thin veneer of civilization, but our emotions have changed but little, and the life cycle remains the same. And that's what folk dancing is all about.

There is but one difference. Dance was once a serious business, not merely created for the entertainment of an audience. Early man had his anxieties just as we have ours. Among the oldest drawings found in Asia are those of dancers done on rock by Paleolithic man. The dance for early man was a means of dealing with his needs and anxieties, of allaying his fear of natural forces—his way of imploring or cajoling the Gods for success at the hunt, fertility, harvest, and of celebrating birth, puberty, marriage, and death. In fact, dance was the earliest form of religion. Later, it was part of the early Christian Mass, and remains a vital part of many religions today. For Chassidim, a Jewish orthodox sect, ecstatic dances are a means of becoming one with their fellowman, with the universe, with God.

8-1: There is no generation gap in folk dancing.

The Complete Dance

We still dance to release tension, and we still folk dance to celebrate the life cycle. Whether it's an Italian Tarantella, an Irish Reel, an Israeli Hora, or a Russian Sher, we are expressing joy through dance, to celebrate a special occasion such as a wedding or a confirmation.

It may come as a surprise to some Americans who think of dance as effeminate that the rest of the world regards it as a manly art. Go to a Greek taverna and watch a line of men holding onto one another's shoulders as they rapturously do a sailor's dance, or a syrtos. Certainly the acrobatic dances performed by Russian men connote virility. To see a line of Yugoslavian men proudly executing intricate steps is to see the embodiment of manliness. And in our own country, the American Indian boy had to learn the dances of his tribe before he was considered worthy as a man. Finally, what did our rugged pioneers do for recreation? Yup! They square danced.

Recently, at a Hungarian folk dance workshop, the leader gave the group some insights into the uses of folk dance. Among other things, it was used in Europe to recruit soldiers. Young men, in smart uniforms, went from village to village performing native folk dances for the villagers. Traditionally, men in uniform who

8-2: Generations of dancers together at the Balkan Arts Center, New York.

dance well seem to attract young women. As soon as the young village men saw the dancing soldiers surrounded by women, they rushed to sign up. Throughout Europe's history of wars and invasions, the vanquished maintained their ethnic identity through songs and dances that reinforced their common nationalistic bond of race, language, music, and traditions. Around a fire at night, soldiers and cavalrymen kept their patriotic fervor at a high pitch just as their progenitors did eons ago, by dancing.

This is not to say that dancing was completely the province of men. Of course women danced too, but demurely, offering no competition to the men.

Today, women and men dancing together still do some of the masculine tradesmen's dances that have come down to us through the centuries. During the Middle Ages, each trade guild, composed of men, had its own distinguishing dances based on its own characteristic movements; farmers, millers, blacksmiths, hunters, tailors, shoemakers all danced about the way they earned their daily bread.

Now that we've proved that folk dance is as much a masculine form of recreational play as it is feminine, it remains to be shown that everybody can dance.

Remember George Gershwin's "I Got Rhythm, I Got Music"? For those people who have been conditioned to think of themselves as "klutzy," (yes, conditioned in childhood by some insensitive adult), rest assured that "you got rhythm, you got music." We breathe in rhythm, walk, chew, copulate, sleep and waken in rhythm. As children, we all dance happily and unself-consciously. Just play some music with a definite beat, turn some little ones loose, then stand back and watch them become intoxicated with the sheer joy of moving in space. Unfortunately, this marvelously free, uninhibited response to music is lost to some of us somewhere between childhood and adulthood. The false notion that dance is an esoteric art for the chosen few becomes reinforced through the growing years.

The First Step

There is no mystery to folk dance. Can you do the following?

walk	run	skip
slide	jump	leap (low and just a little)

8-3: Esther Frankel leading a line in a Yugoslavian dance.

If your answer is "yes," then you can dance, because dance steps are merely combinations of these basic movements. By varying the combinations and rhythm, infinite dance steps and patterns result. For instance, a skip is nothing more than a walk and a hop. If you take one skip and add three walking or running steps, you're dancing a polka. Now put it in reverse—walk three steps and add a hop. You're doing a schottische, a step that occurs in many international dances. What is a waltz? Nothing but a smooth walking step accenting the first step of every three steps taken. Try it.

Left	Right	Left		Right	Left	Right
1	2	3		1	2	3

You're waltzing. Style and movement quality may vary from country to country, yet all folk dances have much in common because the basic steps that are the building blocks remain the same.

Although enjoyment is the primary reason for dancing, an extra bonus is the healthful exercise, the feeling of well-being that accompanies and follows pleasant physical exertion. America is on a health kick. Everyone seems to be in search of a painless way to exercise. All too often we start out in a euphoria of good intentions—sign up at a health club, work out on the machines, or buy high-priced equipment, only to lose interest after a while because we find it has become a bore.

Many of us are turned off by competitive forms of exercise because we fear competition with those who are better coordinated, or have devoted more time to practice than we were able or willing to. For some people, the excitement of competition may be too stressful. Unlike sports, folk dancing doesn't require you to hang in there, win or lose. You can drop out at will. Folk dance is non-competitive; the only competition is with yourself. Satisfaction comes from seeing yourself improve, not from beating anyone. Even if you make some errors while dancing in a circle, it doesn't matter. It's no great loss to a team or to anyone else.

Several years ago at a folk dance festival, our attention was drawn to an attractive young woman, because she appeared spastic. It was distressing to watch her arms and legs flailing about uncontrollably as she danced. Rumor had it that she had suffered brain damage in a bicycle accident, and that her therapist had

8-4: Folk dancing for people of all ages at the Central Unitarian Church in Paramus, New Jersey.

advised folk dance as an adjunct to the therapy she was receiving at the hospital.

Slowly and almost imperceptibly, over the years, we have noticed a marked improvement in the young woman's muscle control. By knowing the steps of many dances in advance, and with the understanding and acceptance she found among her fellow folk dancers, she felt free to make errors, dance off-beat, or out of step. She is still somewhat awkward, but she is no longer spastic. After three years of dancing several nights a week, her coordination has improved enormously. Best of all, she is exercising unselfconsciously while enjoying a social life that might have been denied to her had she not found folk dance. She says, "Folk dance is my thing. It's a trip without acid."

Grace and coordination come with flexibility and muscle strength. A good exercise program should build muscle tone, "oil" the joints, and improve blood circulation. Few exercises can claim to accomplish all three essentials at once. But folk dance can. The importance of the third factor cannot be overstressed. Good blood circulation is the *sine qua non* of good health.

Circulation depends on the ability of the heart to supply sufficient oxygen to the body tissues as the need arises during

8-5: The arts intermingle as an artist captures the dance scene in charcoal.

physical exertion. To accomplish its purpose, an exercise must be vigorous enough to impose stress on the heart. It is interesting that cardiovascular efficiency doesn't depend on age as much as on physiological fitness. So age is no deterrent. It should also be noted that studies have proved that vigorous exercise is a major factor in the prevention of heart attacks and acts as a deterrent to the degenerative effects of aging on the heart and blood vessels.

In addition to being the complete exerciser, folk dance has a unique advantage over other exercises. Unlike monotonous rhythmic exercises repeated over and over (calisthenics, jogging), dancing to the accompaniment of beautiful melodies and interesting rhythms from many lands becomes an aesthetic experience. Because dances are as many and as varied as there are nations on earth, the challenge of learning new dances helps to maintain mental alertness, thus making folk dance a total mind-body experience.

For centuries, dance has been recognized as therapy. From witch doctor to rich doctor, the universal belief that dance has curative powers for some ailments has not changed. The case of Al Matyo, of Cranford, New Jersey, confirms this belief.

"I used to get pains in my legs, so bad that it interfered with my job. You know I have to stand most of the day at work. Well, I finally went to the doctor. He told me that I have fallen arches. I tried all kinds of shoes, and nothing helped. Then the doctor recommended that I try folk dancing. I tried it and got hooked. And well, as you can see . . ." Al is now the leader and teacher of The International Folk Dancers of The Central Unitarian Church of Paramus, New Jersey.

Jackie Higgins, who is the hostess for the group, volunteers, "I was painfully self-conscious and shy. I used to avoid people. Now I enjoy being here with people. I get up and dance and demonstrate dances. I had to talk through my feet before I could be comfortable in conversation. There was a time when I couldn't have talked to you this way."

A Communal Activity

We hear a great deal about alienation in our highly industrialized society. Families and communities have become fragmented. We separate ourselves according to status, age, occupa-

8-6: Al Matyo and Selma Cohen in an Israeli line dance.

8-7: Laszlo leading a performance at a Hungarian festival.

tion, and economic condition. We have even lost the ability to assess people on the basis of character, intelligence, and personality. Perhaps that is why one of the first questions people ask on meeting for the first time is, "What do you do?" A more appropriate question would be, "How do you spend your leisure time?" Because we do tend to socialize with people of our own financial status, religious persuasion, and political convictions, the danger exists that we may lose our vision of the rest of society, and with it, in a sense, a true image of ourselves.

Folk dance is a great equalizer. It cuts across barriers, age differences, nationalities, and occupations. Like a chorus of one hundred singers, each contributing his or her individual voice for the ultimate blending of voices into one beautiful sound, folk dancers in a circle share the enjoyment of moving as one to the same collective rhythm.

What kind of people folk dance? All kinds. A good cross-section of a community can be seen at dance sessions, laughing, conversing, and getting to know one another. People who once considered others as "different," begin to find common ground. Although this doesn't completely alleviate prejudice, it's a step in the right humanitarian direction.

Unlike China, where it is traditional for people of all ages to gather in designated spaces for daily exercise, such as Tai Chi, teenagers in our society are expected to have their own culture, separate and apart from adults. Should a parent attempt to bridge the gap by attempting to do one of the dances currently popular with the adolescent crowd, he or she would be resented, ridiculed, or regarded with benign tolerance. For many families, recreation means an activity away from the rest of the family.

It is refreshing to see families folk dancing together and enjoying one another's company. And when the children are grown, many long-married couples have rekindled the flame, having found this mutual interest. And the elderly find a place where they are welcomed, a place away from the usual senior citizens' groups. It is a common sight to see eighteen-year-olds dancing with people in their sixties and seventies.

Marina Deike, a widowed senior citizen from Upper Montclair, New Jersey, can be seen any Saturday night at the Central Unitarian Church, whirling about the dance floor with partners of all ages. Standing at the refreshment table, she reminisces, "After my husband died, I wanted to die, too. My neighbor insisted that

I come with her and her husband to dance. At first, I refused, thinking, 'I'm too old.' But I feel young here. It has kept me alive. I've made new friends and it's given me a whole new way of life."

The Country Dance Society in Manhattan, New York City, is a more specialized group, but again, it is made up of people of all ages. Russ Houghton, one of the senior members of the organization, can still dance with the best of the young ones. "I've been doing English and related American dances—Welsh and Scottish—for forty-nine years. You know, I met my wife at a summer workshop of The Country Dance Society. We've been dancing in the same group for forty-four years. See Jim Morrison? He's the one up at the mike. He met his wife dancing. Our former director met her husband that way too." With dances such as "Hobbe's Wedding" (every couple kisses before passing on to the next partners), it's easy to see how conducive folk dance is to romance.

According to recent statistics, we have an ever-growing singles population. Consequently, we've been treated to a proliferation of books and articles advising singles about places where social contacts can be made. Most of these places and activities involve the tension of approaching a stranger, and the fear of rejection. It is a great advantage to be able to come to a folk dance class or party without a partner and not feel "out of it." There are no wallflowers at folk dance affairs. The atmosphere is informal and congenial, so it's easy to meet people and make friends. No introductions are necessary. The dancers simply form a circle and make conversation with one another as they wait for the music to start. The use of mixers—sequential partner changing during a dance—helps even the most reticent to get to know everyone in the group.

A youngster, asked to describe folk dance, says, "It gives you a chance to dance with a lot of girls, and just long enough." For men who would like to dance with "a lot of girls," but feel insecure about their ability to lead, that problem never arises. Even in couple dances, routines are learned by both men and women, without one or the other leading. There is true equality of the sexes. A woman may reach out an inviting hand to a man, a gesture to join her in a circle, without feeling uncomfortable or aggressive.

8-8: Oscar Appel dancing in Hungarian costume.

8-9: Members of the Ungaresca in "Csardus."

To further the social possibilities, there are folk festivals, holiday celebrations, workshops, country weekends at camps and hotels, and travel groups—a whole lifestyle. Folk festivals bring together various ethnic groups to taste one another's foods, listen to one another's music, view one another's handicrafts, and hold hands to dance.

Our country has been enriched by a blend of people from all over the world. Some time ago, a group of us visited Van Cortlandt Park in the Bronx. We were happily soaking up the bright spring sunshine when suddenly we heard the distant strains of exotic music. Like sailors drawn to Lorelei's song, we followed the sound, and when the delicious aroma of herbs and roasting meat filled the air, we knew that we had hit paydirt. It wasn't long before we came to a meadow, and there they were—hundreds of Greeks celebrating a Name Day. Several men were busy roasting a lamb on a primitive barbecue they had improvised for the occasion. Other men, dressed in the native short white skirts and white stockings with red pom-poms, danced in a line, the leader twirling a handkerchief above his head, and improvised inspired steps—leaps, turns, and squats. In the background, a line of women danced gracefully, close to the tables that were being set by the older matrons. We all agreed that we felt as if we had been transported to an ancient island in Greece. Paradoxically, the festivals we had traveled great distances to see in Europe were ersatz, staged for tourists; this one, in New York City, was authentic. Captivated by the entire scene, we joined a line for a hasopikos, thinking we'd go unnoticed in the crowd. But such was not the case. As soon as the music stopped, we were surrounded by smiling faces, plied with questions about our knowledge of Greek dances, and hospitably welcomed to join in the feast.

To add to all of its other advantages, folk dance is one of the few bargains left in our highly inflated economy. No special equipment is needed, just a comfortable pair of shoes. For men, slacks or dungarees and a light shirt; for women, a skirt that allows for movement, or pants, and a loose blouse. At parties and festivals, many people don beautifully embroidered ethnic clothes and jewelry they've collected in their travels or bought at booths during festivals. Most groups charge a small fee, ranging from $.25 at universities to $2.50, including refreshments and

8-10: Al Matyo announcing the next dance.

teaching. When school playgrounds and parks are used, there is no fee. The following is just a random sampling of free outdoor activities:

In New York City, every Sunday during the summer, everyone is welcome to join the dancing in Central Park, outside the Delacorte Theatre, starting around 2:00 p.m. and continuing until sunset. In San Diego, California, folk dancing takes place in Balboa Park on Sundays. Private and public groups perform at the annual festival. Fort Wayne, Indiana, has square dancing outdoors in city parks. Mobile, Alabama, holds a spring music and folk dance festival.

Tastes vary, and folk dance has something for everybody. By and large, square dancing seems to be more popular in many parts of the United States, simply because it is our heritage. Our early settlers brought their dances from the mother country, Great Britain. Contras like the Virginia Reel, performed with partners in two straight lines, are equally popular in New England and the South. Throughout the Southwest, where Spanish culture left its mark, Spanish colonial dances are favored. In Solvang, California, Danish-Americans celebrate by performing Danish dances. The "Running Set" of Appalachia is the legacy of early Scottish settlers, just as southern clogging is the legacy of Ireland. Throughout the country round dances, a combination of folk and ballroom steps, are performed to both popular and folk tunes. Any or all of the foregoing may be on the program at an evening of international folk dancing.

Once started, folk dance not only becomes a lifetime interest, but it can open whole new vistas. Some people have even used the dance as a springboard for new careers. Those with a bent toward learning more about past civilizations have gone on to study anthropology. Pearl Primus, the famous dancer and choreographer, became an anthropologist and a college professor. Those who are sensitive to people with emotional and physical problems have become dance therapists. Some have opened stores specializing in folk dance records, books, clothes, and shoes. Others organize and lead specialized trips to European countries, stopping at out-of-the-way hamlets where village life has hardly been touched by the twentieth century. *Folk Dance Directory* and *Viltis*, the oldest national folk dance magazine, are products of ardent folk dancers with a penchant for creative writing. Some fine jewelry and costume designers started out as folk dancers.

Rick Leighton, who dances with The Country Dance Society in New York City, sums up the possibilities:

"I used to be a serious, introverted kind of guy. I needed to let off steam. One of my friends took me along to dance. I've

8-11: Generations.

8-12: Oscar Appel, Sheila Brenin: Russian Ballroom Dance.

always loved music, and I was immediately taken with the dancing. Also, the people I met were the friendliest imaginable. This really helped me out of my shell. Eventually, I joined a performing group and started to teach folk dance. Then, when I went into the computer field, I carried over some of the techniques I had learned from teaching dance to my teaching at IBM, and subsequently to my teaching on college level. I owe much of my ability to deal with people in business and professionally to folk dancing."

Whether people become folk dancers because of a cultivated aesthetic sense, or conversely, cultivate an aesthetic sense as a result of their appreciation for folk music and dance, it is hardly by coincidence that these same people meet one another at museums, concerts, the ballet, poetry readings, and at environmental protection organizations. A common denominator seems to be a love of beauty and nature, and a respect for all living things.

As our life expectancy increases, and as we move along to a shorter work-week and early retirement, more people will be looking for a constructive lifetime interest to fill leisure time. Unfortunately, our schools prepare us for a profession or a vocation, but do little to educate us for the intelligent use of leisure time. It is left to us to find the way by trial and error.

If folk dance can promote physical, mental, and social growth, without regard to sex, age, or economic status, and if it can give us an appreciation of other cultures, then it is the ideal recreational activity.

Twentieth-century technology has bridged the farthest reaches of our planet, fusing it into one interdependent community. If folk dance can cement individual and community relationships, is it too much to hope that it can act as a link for friendship and brotherhood with the rest of mankind?

chapter 9

The Game

by Bernie DeKoven

The only conclusion that can be reached from reading a book about play is that we need to do more than read if we want to share the experience.

In this chapter, I've considered a number of different approaches to sharing play. I've begun with a consideration of the largest issue I could think of—the relationship between the search for play and the development of a healthy culture. This piece is written to provide a rationale because there are times when we need to be able to explain.

The rest of the chapter explores different stages of the process of sharing play—from playing by yourself to playing with thousands.

All of the pieces express, in one way or another, the vision that has led to the publication of this book: we need to play, we need to find as many ways as possible to do something about it.

Cultures and Competitions

Children play with everything they can find: string, pots, boxes, seeds, marbles. This is universal. There are other qualities of play that seem to be universal: the demand for fairness, the need for a challenge, the delight in taking risks, the desire for control, the pleasure of total engagement.

Certain kinds of play seem to coincide more with the cultural norms than others. Hence, each culture tends to promote one kind of play over another, to encourage certain kinds of risks and challenges more than others.

For most of the children in our culture, the play forms in which we compete against each other are more favored than those in which we cooperate. Our children, when they are just entering school, bring with them every sort of play activity they can find. They play hand-clapping games like paddycake, dancing games like ring-around-a-rosy, dramatic games like house. They also play hunting games like tag and hide-and-seek, racing games, soft war games like tug of war and king of the mountain.

Our particular culture has been divided, somehow, into male and female. In the male culture, games of interpersonal competition are more favored. The logic of this seems to belong to a slightly older form of our culture in which men compete with each other for material control. A winner in the male culture is one who has the most control over money. Men are set against each other as they enter the working world to engage in what amounts to a total economic war.

The traditional female culture is characterized more by cooperation than by competition. Women are encouraged to be good mothers. Being a good mother is not competitive. Women don't win by being better mothers than other women. They win by maintaining the household. Thus, girls' games differ from boys' games—not originally, but eventually, as the culture is able to exert more influence. Girls play paddycake, jump-rope, singing and dancing and dramatic games. Boys play marbles, they wrestle and race.

In a study by Brian Sutton-Smith, J. M. Roberts and R. M. Kozella (*The Study of Games*, Avedon and Sutton-Smith, Wiley, 1969, pp. 488-496), girls and boys were invited to play tic-tac-toe. It was found that the girls who consistently won the game were also "hyperactive, impulsive, aggressive and a tomboy." In other words, they had moved towards a male culture. Girls who consistently had draws in the games were also not interested in aggression or gross motor games. Sutton-Smith sums up this finding by saying that "the good girl plays it safe."

These findings are bothersome. Our cultural values—at least the ones which we seem most eager to pass on—are not unified. Tomboys (winning girls) and sissies (drawing boys) are deviants from the norm. They have adopted the wrong set of values. And yet, it is clear to many of us that we can't continue to nurture this distinction and maintain a whole culture. Because we wish to establish a new norm, we find ourselves having to create new games.

Other cultures have different norms. In general, it turns out that those cultures in which survival is the key issue tend to select more cooperative play forms. The competition must be against nature rather than against people.

One of the most common games in Alaska and Australia is that of cat's cradle. It is a game of pure cooperation, the goal being to arrive together at a complex figure. Some hunting and target-throwing games are also popular, and though players are competing, it is clearly a different kind of competition than that characterized by such games as football and hockey. The skills developed are not used against each other but against a neutral object, like a target. As training for survival, these games are clearly between man and nature, as opposed to, in the Western cultures, between man and man.

In some cultures, the demand for cooperation takes on almost compulsive characteristics. K. O. L. Burridge, in *MAN*, (June, 1957, pp. 88-89) describes the game of taketak played by the Tangu people of New Guinea.

First of all, he explains that "the notion of moral equality between persons . . . receives primary expression in the attempt to exchange equivalent amounts of foodstuffs—a task entailing almost insuperable practical difficulties and rarely explicitly attained except by mutual consent and agreement."

Taketak is played by two teams. Each team has the same number of spinning tops. When the first player goes, his objective is to spin the top and throw it into a pile of spines made from coconut palm fronds, striking as many spines as possible. Those spines which are struck are removed. Then it is the second team's turn. After a round, the spines are counted. If one team has struck more spines than the other, the lesser amount is returned to the pile of the team that hit more spines. The game continues in this manner until, somehow, both teams after completing a round have *exactly the same amount* of spines in each of their piles. Since this is often impossible to arrange for, frequently the game stops when both teams simply give up.

All of this scholarly-type information leads to some significant hypotheses:

1. Cooperative games are more meaningful in some cultures than others.

2. Cooperation, as well as competition, can be taken to an extreme.

3. Sexism, in our culture, has led to the formation of two separate cultures, one female and emphasizing cooperation, the other male and emphasizing competition.

What is significant about these hypotheses is the logical conclusion that we would be better off, if our purpose is to create a wise and balanced culture, acknowledging the value of cooperation for boys as much as we have begun to accept the positive value of competition for girls. We must be careful in this shifting of emphasis to be moderate, to provide a wide variety of acceptable play forms so that we may create a culture which embraces the wide variety of skills and characteristics of its members.

Right in Your Own Backyard
or Your Attic, or Your Basement,
or the Street

The Idea We can play anywhere. We like playing. We like sharing play. We'd like to share play in as many places and as many ways and with as many people as possible.

The Principle The more the merrier. The more games, the more different kinds of games, the more people, the more different kinds of people, the merrier the merriment.

The Guarantee It's going to take time. It's going to be different each time we do it. If the idea is that we want to share play, if the principle is to provide each other with as many ways to share play as we can, we're bound to have a good time together. It has to work.

Preparation Find as many people as we can who want to share in making the event with us. The more people who work with us so that we can play together, the more shared, the more effective the event will be. If we start out together, we'll wind up even more together. Let's talk about play together. Let's play together and find out how we like playing best.

Equipment There are two basic alternatives: little and lots. With little equipment, we have to organize people. With lots of equipment, we have to organize things. What kinds of things? If we have things that we are going to worry about—expensive games, irreplaceable sets—then we're going to spend more time worrying than playing. If we have junk, we can spend more time playing. What kind of junk? Lots. Like a hundred cardboard boxes, twenty-five pounds of rubber bands, five gallons of bubble-making solution, water, sand, styrofoam scraps, paint, old clothes. If the stuff we use can be used in lots of ways, we have even more. Cardboard cartons can be made into giant building blocks, into houses and mazes, giant checkers, obstacle courses. Rubber bands can be linked into chains. The chains can be stretched everywhere. They can be woven and twanged. They can make music. If the stuff is messy, confine it to a clean-upable area. Get everybody to bring in their favorite junk. Magazines for collages, make-up, paper for origami and airplane making. And then, maybe, some balls, a parachute, if there's the room, borrowed stuff from schools and friends. Kazoos, balloons.

Food   Ask people to bring food to share. Salad-fixings, sandwich-makings, veggies. Start a kettle of boiling water and take turns adding soup-type elements. Rabbi Zalman Schachter tells this story: Once, a great rabbi was invited to visit hell and heaven. He decided to go to hell first. There he saw a large table. On the table was every possible gourmet item known to modern civilization. The damned were standing around the table—each with a rod tied to his back and another rod tied to his arms. And though they had forks in each hand, they couldn't get the food to their mouths. A true hell. Then the rabbi went to heaven. There he saw a large table. On the table was every possible gourmet item known to modern civilization. The blessed were standing around the table—each with a rod tied to his back and another rod tied to his arms. And though they couldn't get food in their mouths, they were rejoicing and delighting. Why? Because they were feeding each other. This is the difference between heaven and hell. So, make a heavenly meal. Have people feed each other.

Drink   Play and alcohol don't seem to mix very well. Fill a juicer with bizarre, health-producing items. Fill the site with bizarre, health-producing people.

The Invitation   Find the people who want to play with you. Convincing doesn't help. Being there is the most convincing

9-1: A moment of one-shoed grace on a rope swing.

thing. Those people will bring others next time.

The Place   Anywhere. Change the place for each event, because each place has its own rules, its own character. The more places you play together in, the more the togetherness is felt.

The People   Everybody. Young. Old. Handicapped. The more different kinds of people we play with, the deeper and bigger the sense of play.

The Time   When it's convenient. When it's easy for people to take the time. Dinner-time. Weekends. A couple of hours, a couple of days. The more time, the better.

Starting   So, now we've got the people and the things and the food and whatever else we decided to try out. So, how do we start? Easy. We play anything with anybody around. Since some of us have played together, we already have an idea of some things to play. Maybe we start out playing by ourselves. All we need to do is make sure that other people know that it's OK to join. So, we make it known. We invite. We don't insist, we ask. And then, when there are enough people to keep that thing going (volleyball, maybe, or face-painting, or charades, or whatever), then we go and start another game with whoever is around to play with us.

The Arts   Because we're playing together, because we're making it up as we go along, we're being creative. Creativity and play are part of the same feeling—freedom and wholeness. So, we make instruments out of wooden blocks, combs and tissue paper, and we play music. Norman Berger invented a string art game. He gets a lot of kite string and draws with it by laying it out on grass (the greener the better, says Norman). Then he gets ladders so people can see what they've made together. Or, maybe we get a spotlight and hang it straight down so that we make a circle of light—instant stage.

Donations   If it takes money to make it happen, ask for money to keep it going. If you don't get any money, do it for free next time. If you do get money, well, buy some frisbees or whatever. If money's a hard thing to come by, trade things—games, toys, whatever.

Ending It   Clean up together. See, when people take responsibility for caring for the place as well as for the people, well, they feel that they own the event a little more. It's like what happens when you go over to somebody's house for dinner. If you just sit around and wait to get served, you feel like a stranger, a guest. If you help with the meal and the dishes, you feel like you're home. It's easier to play when you feel at home. Asking people to help clean is helping them play, too. Doing it together, everybody, makes the event more than play—it makes it real.

Resources Junk is everywhere. It's the one thing our society has been able to create with consummate ease. Factories have junk. Carpet places have long cardboard tubes for giant pick-up sticks, for obstacle courses and castle turrets. Shoe factories have leather scraps. Newspapers have ends of rolls which are good for murals.

Games are everywhere, too. Your best resource is people. Ask kids, ask everybody to teach each other games. How many ways are there to play checkers? Use old games to make up new ones. Monopoly pieces for a scavenger hunt, money for a pretend auction. Magazines for collages. Newspaper for papier-mache. Egg cartons. Sticks for stilts. String for cat's cradle. Or go to the library and look up some old game books. More games than you could use in twenty years of play.

Love . . . is what it's all about, not play, really. The event is meaningful because people feel meaningful doing it, because it's an act of unity and community. Don't worry about the games. They come from the joy of sharing anything.

New Games from Old

Let's start from an old game and see how we can make it new.

First of all, we'll have to find an old game that we all want to play together. That's the first step in making the game new—finding one that everybody wants to play. Already, the game stops being so old. Already there's a newness to it. It's not like we're walking into the middle of a game that's already going. It's not like we're looking for the game we should be playing this season. It's a whole new thing, this deciding what game we want to play together.

It's new, but it's not strange. There were times before when we had a lot of games to choose from—when we made the choice together. Times before when the game felt new.

Let's say that at least this time dodgeball might be the right game for us. We could even call it New Dodgeball if we wanted,

9-2: An experiment in back-to-back dodgeball.

seeing that it's the first time we decided to play it together. It's new to us, at least.

It turns out that there are a lot of different ways to play dodgeball. This is a little disturbing. Just when we were feeling good about finally finding a game that everybody wanted to play we discover that we haven't come to a clear agreement. Different people were talking about different dodgeball games.

One of us thought that we were going to play against the wall. The way she knows how to play dodgeball, everybody but one stands up against the wall. The player who is "it" stands about twenty feet away from the wall and tries to hit everybody else. The players against the wall can move as far as the left and right boundaries. Anybody hit becomes "it," too. The game goes on until only one player is left to throw at. That player starts the next game.

Another thought that the game was played in a big rectangle with everybody inside except for two enders. The enders start with the ball and throw the ball back and forth trying to hit the people inside. Anyone hit goes out of the game and can't play again until the next game. The last two people in are enders for the next round.

Another thought that the game was played in a big circle, with half the team inside and half the team out. The people on the outside were trying to hit the people on the inside. Anybody hit changed places with the outsider that hit him.

Another remembers playing it in a circle, but with different rules.

Another remembers a game with maybe a dozen balls going at the same time.

On the other hand, it's not so bad, really, that we haven't come to an agreement yet. We have at least agreed on the general theme of the game—people trying to hit each other with a ball. And having all those different ways of pursuing that theme, well, it gives us more to choose from. That's a help.

Actually, we're more interested in getting started. There's no way, really, that we can be absolutely sure which game is going to be the one that everybody *really* wants to play.

So we decide, being just slightly arbitrary, that we'll play the wall variation.

We find a nice wall, set up the right and left boundaries (shoes make good boundary markers), we choose who's going to be "it," and then we start the game. Except that we can only find a basketball to play with.

Some of us don't feel that safe having a basketball thrown at them. They'd rather play with a softer ball. They are having remarkably deep-felt visions of broken noses. We agree, since that's the only ball around, that the thrower has to aim between knees and feet only.

Once again, we've made the game new. We did it by adding a rule that allowed everybody to feel safe enough to play.

All right, now we've got the game going. Finally. It's beginning to pick up a rhythm of its own. We're getting into it. We're feeling good. Yeah, this is the right game. Good choice.

Fifteen rounds later, we're still enjoying the game. Nobody got hurt. Some of us made some very smooth dodges—others some really fine throws. We're getting better at it, too. The good plays seem to be happening more often.

Truth is, we've just about had it.

Only this time, when Alice throws the ball at Bernard, Bernard, instead of dodging, catches the ball and throws it at Alice. He misses. Alice gets the ball and throws it to Charlie. Charlie catches it and tries to hit Bernard. Bernard dodges. David retrieves and tries to hit Evelyn.

All of a sudden there are no sides. There are no clear rules. There doesn't even seem to be an objective to the game at all. People are just throwing the ball, to or at whomever they want. When somebody gets hit, nothing seems to happen to anybody. No roles are changed. Nobody goes out. Clearly something is dodgeball-like about what we're doing together. But what are we playing?

Two things are obvious: one—people are cheating; two—nobody seems to care. What is happening, in fact, is that the game is getting new again. It had been on the verge of becoming old. Some of us had begun to tire, to feel not good enough to play. So, we changed the game. We made it new again.

And then, Frank runs to the car and brings back another basketball, and proceeds to throw it at George. Meanwhile, George has made a ball out of his jacket. He throws it to Harriet. Harriet catches it and tries to hit Bernard. Instead, she gets hit by Isabelle's socks.

Jerry, sensitive chap that he is, realizes that the game is approaching mayhem. Though it is fun, he has already caught himself thinking about throwing his rings at someone. He realizes that things are close to getting out of hand.

Conveniently for everybody, Jerry knows that the game needs to be kept safe. He can already sense that some people are beginning to cower more than dodge. And, conveniently for the subject of this article, Jerry is the one who knows the game where people throw a dozen balls at the same time. That game is called bombardment.

He stops the old dodgeball game and suggests the new one. Again the game is made new.

Yes, it's still dodgeball, and yes, it's a form of dodgeball that others have played. But, again, it's new for the people who are playing. It's better than what they were playing before—not because it's a better game, but because it's more in keeping with how everybody seems to want to play.

The fact is, we could play dodgeball forever. We could always keep it new.

Obviously, it isn't important that the game is different. What makes a new game valuable is that it allows the players to play the way they want to. What makes a new game really new is that it is always subject to change. What makes the change meaningful is that it helps us play the way we like playing.

Dodgeball is a very simple game. First of all, there are only two roles: shooter and target. The shooter wants to hit the target, and the target wants to avoid getting hit.

Second, there is usually a separation between the areas which "belong" to the shooter and the areas which "belong" to the target.

The size of the areas, the number of players in each role, the object thrown, the number of objects thrown, the goal of the shooter or target, what happens as a result of success are all variables which we can change without ever stopping playing dodgeball.

Size of Areas   The less room for the target, the easier it is for the shooter; the less room for the shooter, the easier it is for the target. So, if people are getting hit too easily to make the game fun, increase their area and decrease the shooter's area.

Number   The more shooters, the more difficulty for the target, and the more difficulty for one particular shooter to succeed; the more targets, the easier it is for the shooter and the more

9-3: Multiball dodgeball.

difficult for the shooter to hit a particular target.

Object Thrown   The heavier the object, the more difficult to throw and the more threatening for the target; the lighter the object, the more difficult to control and the less threatening to the target. Thus, perhaps playing dodgeball with a bowling ball would prove somehow less than satisfying for those at whom the ball is thrown. On the other hand, playing with a balloon may be simply too frustrating—especially if it is filled with helium. An interesting compromise could be reached through the use of water-filled balloons.

Number of Objects   The more objects, the easier for the shooter and the more difficult for the target.

Nature of Boundaries   Playing in a circle is different from playing against a wall. First of all, you have to worry more about the ball getting lost. Second of all, it provides the opportunity for the shooters to surround the targets. Bombardment is played in four adjoining rectangles comprising one large rectangle. The game begins with the two teams facing each other in the middle rectangles. If a player from team A hits a player from team B, the B-player goes into the area behind the A team. Now if the B-player catches the ball, he can throw it at the A team from the other side of their territory. Thus, eventually, both teams wind up surrounded by the other team.

Success   The smaller the target, the more difficult to hit. The longer a player is in the role of target, the greater are his chances of getting hit. Is it a reward or a punishment to be a target? Do you want to play so that if you hit someone you get to be a target, too? How about if when you're a target, if you can catch the ball you get to become a shooter?

Result of Success   The target may be out of the game if hit, she might exchange roles with the shooter, she may be assigned to a different area. The same, naturally, applies to the shooter.

Given all of these variables, it is possible to arrive at at least a hundred new games. What really makes the game new is that we can change it.

Free-Form Frisbee Golf

We begin with one of your basic insights on the nature of frisbees and their relationship to the spirit of humankind: it's fun to watch a frisbee go.

Now, I grant you that this basic insight is not of very significant spiritual impact. It doesn't seem to carry the same force as some of your more profound truths. Should you, in your quest for illumination, be told by the Great Guru himself that it's fun to watch a frisbee go, you would probably experience that truth as markedly less than relevant.

On the other hand, it is enough of a basic insight to lead you to a most delightful play experience.

Let us, therefore, examine this basic insight in greater depth.

Having accepted the fact that it's fun to watch a frisbee go, you take your frisbee, throw it, and watch it go. Ah, yes, indeed, this is fun. Unfortunately, it is also true that the frisbee stops. This, quite clearly, is not fun.

You could purchase, or otherwise acquire, a multitude of frisbees, and thereby extend your opportunity to delight in the flight in direct proportion to the number of frisbees available. But this strategy is somewhat less than satisfying. The expense, first of all, seems to dampen the spirit of play. And then there's the environmental pollution caused by indiscriminate frisbee proliferation.

9-4: Teeing off in frisbee golf.

A somewhat more practical solution is to go where the frisbee has rested, remove it, and throw it again.

After several years of doing this, even the most playful of attitudinal modes tends to take on a quality of boredom. Something is clearly lacking.

A discovery of some practical as well as aesthetic value, therefore, occurs when you find that you can actually direct the flight of the frisbee to some location which will assure easier access. It becomes evident that it is less desirable that the frisbee land in a tree or on the roof or upon a passing vehicle or person, and consequently more desirable that the frisbee land in an open or accessible space. This discovery leads you to ascribe more value to those flights of the frisbee which enhance access.

Thus is born the desire to take aim. The clearly positive reinforcement you acquire from having the frisbee land where you would like it to land adds significantly to the overall value of the frisbee experience. You can now take pleasure in a successful landing as well as in a joyous flight. This, clearly, leads to a manifestation of a basic insight of even more profound impact.

As you discover the experience of accuracy, you will be interested in doubling your pleasure. This is definitely desirable. You can now select to appreciate either the grace of the flight or the exactitude of the landing. Thus, should the frisbee, as a result of the impartial factors of wind and other natural phenomena, fail to land where you desire, you can still appreciate the flight. And the logical converse of an uninspiring flight but delightful landing also can provide you with the opportunity to appreciate.

At this juncture, the soul's unrest makes available still more intriguing probabilities. There is manifest a marked tendency to shrink the target. Thus, having the frisbee land anywhere within three acres of the general direction of the throw actually becomes less satisfying than having the frisbee land within three inches.

Simultaneously, another dialectic is born. You wish not only to narrow the target, but also to arrive at that target by means of an inspiring flight. In other words, the well-thrown frisbee becomes an ever more exacting and illusive experience.

Lest we conclude that this is due to some perversity within the human psyche, allow me to point out that this development is purely logical. After each flight, you are confronted with the need to retrieve the frisbee. Since you wish to enjoy the flight as well as conserve effort in the act of retrieval, you naturally appreciate those landings which result in easier access. Too, because you wish to experience an inspiring flight, you find that sacrificing that flight for the sake of mere expedience is soul-shrinking and contrary to purpose. But the stage of most profound illumination occurs only when logic itself is defeated. When perversity finally wins out, one is led to THE GAME.

For example, you throw the frisbee. The flight is lovely, but due to circumstances clearly beyond your control, the frisbee lands a few meters away from the target. Out of sheer and mindless perversity, yes, perversity, you pick up the frisbee from its landing place and, standing exactly on that spot, throw it those several meters to the previously designated target.

Clearly, this is perverse. If you were to be logical, you would simply bow before the forces of fortune and select a new target. To insist on getting the frisbee to the original target is pure stubbornness. It's only a few meters away. The flight from here to there is obviously of insignificant duration. Yet, one does not find satisfaction until the frisbee gets there.

And yet, perverse though it may seem, it is a stroke of genius. It results in the creation of the game.

What game? Why, frisbee golf, naturally. You merely select a target and attempt to get the frisbee there in the *fewest possible throws.* Thus, the throwing place becomes the tee, the target the hole, and all is well. Even if the frisbee misses, the chance of getting it there increases favorably after each throw. Sooner or later, satisfaction is guaranteed.

Unfortunately, there are still issues to be resolved. Granted that frisbee and golf is a good combination, granted that it is satisfying of your essential perversity, what about the par?

In order to deal with this burning issue, since par has not yet been established, it must be created. Thus, when you attempt to get the frisbee from here to there, you must also decide, before the throw itself, a criterion for satisfaction.

The question becomes: how many throws (strokes) need you execute in getting the frisbee from here to there before you admit failure? This is, indeed, a soul-wrencher.

And yet another question arises: to whom do you ascribe the authority to declare par?

Fortunately, there is protocol. In golf, par is fixed by those who design the course. Since, in the process of playing, you are in fact designing the course as you go along, par-fixing is simply left to the discretion of the player.

Behold: Free-form frisbee golf is born:

Official Rules: The Game For One

1. Decide where you want to get the frisbee to and from (tee and hole location).
2. Decide how many throws it should take to get you there (par).
3. Stand on tee and throw frisbee holeward.
4. In case you haven't scored a hole-in-one, pick up the frisbee where it landed. Stand exactly on that spot. Throw again.
5. When you finally make it, decide where else you want to throw to.

The game rises to a manifold poetic excellence when several people are playing at the same time.

Official Rules of Free-Form Frisbee Golf for a Few

1. Give each player a frisbee of differentiable color.
2. Follow steps one and two of the game for one. All players must agree on hole location, tee placement and par.
3. Take turns following steps three and four of the game for one.
4. When everybody has attained the hole, decide collectively the next hole, tee and par.

Some Intriguing Ramifications

1. A frisbee may land in the "rough" (in the middle of a pond, on the roof, etc.).
   A. Must one shoot from that spot?
   B. Is one allowed any leeway? Could one place only one foot or other bodily extremity on the landing place and still execute a fair throw?
2. A frisbee may land upside down or on its edge.
   A. Should one be rewarded or penalized for such landing?
   B. Should the reward or penalty be ascribed to one or both players?

It is recommended that when you encounter such intriguing ramifications, any decision or rule-making should only be allowed to apply after that event. Thus, if it is the case that my frisbee has landed in quicksand, any new rule covering a quicksand landing should not be made to apply to the first advent. It is further recommended that general agreement on the use of common sense be made prior to the commencement of the game—especially when playing in quicksand.

On the other hand, it is highly possible that free-form frisbee golf evolved in a less logical manner. One or two people might have sat around one day, and, finding themselves within a golf course and without golf equipment and with frisbees. . . . Or, some scholar might have thought up the game, all by herself, in pursuit of a broader philosophical issue, such as: how does one play golf outside of a golf course?

This leads me to speculate on the possibilities of free-form frisbee polo, free-form frisbee bowling, croquet, and, in extreme cases, perhaps you might even be led to wonder about playing some kind of catch with the frisbee. Who knows, it might be fun.

Playing Together

Ping-Pong   How many ways are there to play ping-pong?

According to most people, there is only one real way. Real ping-pong is a game you win when you can make your opponent miss.

Billy Doran is getting a ping-pong table. He has always liked the game. But, winning ping-pong was never enough for him. He really felt good about the game only when he was playing hard. He liked it best when he found himself making spectacular shots. And he liked the game even more when his opponent made spectacular returns.

That was the real reason he wanted a ping-pong table—not so that he could beat everybody in the neighborhood, but so that he could find people who enjoyed playing as hard as he did. He wasn't looking for people to play against. He was looking for people to play with.

He hasn't gotten the table yet. First, he has to build an addition to his house so that he has room for it. Obviously, he regards ping-pong as something important enough to invest that much into. In the meantime, until he finishes the addition, he's practicing the game.

Whenever he has the chance, he looks for someone with a ping-pong table who likes to play hard. What they do together is most remarkable.

It doesn't seem right, almost, to say that they are playing ping-pong. What they are doing is playing ping-pong together. Ping-pong is the thing they're using to make it happen.

Actually, they are just volleying. Their game, if that's what it is, has a different kind of goal. In fact, the game is completely pointless.

On the other hand, they seem to be focusing as hard as if they were playing a real game. They've been volleying for over an hour. Whenever the ball goes off the table, they both seem a little disappointed. And, when the ball gets going again, a curious harmony begins to get established. Somehow, the ball seems to pick up speed. Both players become more active, more intent, just trying to get the ball back to each other. Some of the shots they are making are indeed spectacular. Several times, one or both of them laughs in amazement at what they have made the ball do.

They each know what the other's best shot is. Billy likes distance. Bernie favors his backhand. So, that's what they try to give each other—the opportunity to make the best possible shot. In fact, there is no way to tell who is the better player. Both of them seem to be occupied in the same pursuit. They each enjoy playing hard. But their efforts, their real victory, is one which they can only win together.

What they are doing makes sense. After all, no matter what rules they use, it takes two to play the game. No matter what perspective we take, the game is something that is played together.

But are they playing ping-pong? Have they discovered another way to play the game or have they made up a new game?

The fact is, it doesn't matter what we call it. What game they are playing doesn't seem to matter. What matters is that they have found a way to play together, and, in the process, they have discovered that they like it better, that it is more rewarding for each of them—a more significant achievement—and that asking which one of them is the better player is like asking whether sunshine is better than rain or eating better than sleeping. The real point of pointless ping-pong is that it works.

What they have found is that playing together is different from playing against each other. That, in itself, is a major discovery. Before, there was only one way to play ping-pong. Now there are two. It certainly makes the game a better investment.

Billy's discovery has led him through a whole series of wonderfully obvious insights. He has learned that playing with people is, in fact, more rewarding than playing against them. He likes the feeling better. It lasts longer. In fact, it works better.

When Billy played regulation ping-pong he found fewer and fewer people he could play against. He got better at the game, and what getting better did for him was to make it harder and harder to find people to play against. The better his game, the less chance he could find to play it.

Now he can play with anyone who wants to play with him. Sure, sometimes the game is gentler, sometimes harder, but it doesn't matter, really, because in either event he gets to play. And playing gently is also good.

And sometimes, playing with the wrong hand is good. And sometimes, just trying to keep the ball off the table is good. And sometimes playing with two paddles. And sometimes, running around the table, or playing underneath it, or playing against the walls, or playing without a net or without a paddle is good, is good, is good.

So, when Billy finishes building his addition, he's going to get a ping-pong table.

And the answer to the question of the day: How many ways are there to play ping-pong?

As many people as there are to play ping-pong with.

Socks   I am the proud owner of forty-three different socks. No, not forty-three different pairs of socks. Forty-three different socks: socks that are the same color but of different pattern; socks that are of the same pattern but of different size; socks that are of the same texture, but different material. Research into this phenomenon has led me to the discovery that I am not the only one upon whom the laundering process has bestowed this legacy.

Others, unfortunately, are not as proud as I of this possession. Most tend to regard the presence of solitaire socks as tokens of disorder—invasion by the merciless forces of chaos.

Solitaire socks have become a source of pride for me because I have discovered that socks can be caught and thrown with remarkable ease and accuracy. By taking two or three socks and

9-5: A poly-Schmerltz launch.

balling them up and carefully tucking the ball into the top of one of the socks, I have created a genuine play device.

I call this device "the sock-ball."

A sock-ball has sufficient weight to be thrown gracefully. It is of sufficient softness to allow for hard throwing without fear of extensive damage to the person to whom one throws. Intensive research has led me to the discovery that damage to objects of moderate fragility is negligible. In other words, it seems that the sock-ball is one of the finest play devices available to modern man. It is, perhaps, what the world has been waiting for.

Question: How can I keep my sock-ball from unraveling?

Answer: It is a vain pursuit. Sock-balls unravel. Such is their nature. If they did not unravel, they would not be what we have come to understand as true sock-balls. My recommendation is that you try one of the following rule modifications:

A. The object of the game is to keep the sock-ball in motion, throwing it back and forth, until it has completely unraveled.

B. The object is to keep the sock-ball aloft, and, when it has fully unraveled, that each player catch one of the component socks before any strike the ground.

C. When a sock-ball unravels, one must put a fully raveled sock-ball into play without breaking the rhythm of the game.

Question: I have noticed that my sock-ball doesn't bounce. What, if anything, can be done to give it a more elastic property?

Answer: My first recommendation is that you avoid games that call for bouncing things. The non-bounciness of sock-balls should not be construed as a negative quality. In closed quarters or areas of human density, non-bounciness is a positive asset. However, should you wish to put more bounce in your sock-ball, it can be done quite easily by inserting an old tennis ball into one of the socks.

Comment: Isn't placing tennis balls inside one's sock-balls a violation of the spirit of sock-ball making?

Retort: It can be rightly considered such. Old tennis balls, however, lie within the tradition of sock-balls insofar as they are what one might call throw-out-resistant. They are more frequently assigned to storage rather than refuse areas.

9-6: A Schmerltz launching.

9-7: Group juggling.

Aside: Interestingly enough, the tennis ball/sock combination has been used most effectively in the creation of Peter Whiteley's famous throwing object, the Schmerltz. Though the recommended Schmerltz is made by dropping a ball into a tube sock and then tying a knot in the sock area immediately above the ball, I have found that actually any sock will do. I do not like to discriminate among socks. The Schmerltz is then taken out to a large, open area, and thrown into the air (this is accomplished most satisfactorily by holding on to the end of the sock in which the ball is not, twirling it about or near one's head, and then tossing it enthusiastically). A Schmerltz catch seems to be more of a significant achievement when it is performed upon the ball-less end of the sock only. On the other hand, it is a pleasant enough pastime to merely launch Schmerltzes indiscriminately for the pure pleasure of appreciating their flight. Unfortunately, it need be noted that the Schmerltz doesn't bounce very well, either.

Question: How many socks does it take to make a sock-ball?

Answer: I, myself, prefer the two-sock sock-ball. I have, however, toyed with sock-balls in excess of seven socks. It is rumored that a seven-sock sock-ball has a more spectacular, and hence, more profound, unraveling effect.

Question: Do you recommend that the brighter socks be placed outside or inside the sock-ball?

Answer: Consider it an opportunity for self-expression. At times, a dark sock-ball is infinitely more appropriate than a bright one.

Question: Is there a particular game which you find most suited to the sock-ball medium?

Answer: Actually no. I have found that even basketball can be played with the sock-ball. Of course, dribbling is somewhat unsatisfactory. Instead, I recommend that the rule be either that you must roll the sock-ball on the floor until you are ready to make your shot, or that you must keep the sock-ball in the air. In either event, basketsock-ball is pleasant enough.

The games which seem to require the least modification, however, are those which call for throwing and catching. Juggling is one of the most profoundly stirring of sock-ball events. Group juggling is one of the most enjoyable forms of juggling.

Question: How do you play sock-ball group juggling?

Answer: First of all, you need several sock-balls, and approximately as many people. At first, one sock-ball is tossed around so that each player has caught and thrown it one time. The player who starts out the game should be the last player to receive the sock-ball. When this cycle has been completed, the group should attempt to repeat the process exactly, each person throwing to the person to whom he has thrown before, catching it from the one from whom he caught it before. After the pattern of catch and throw is firmly established, another member of the group might introduce a new sock-ball into the pattern. Thus, both sock-balls get thrown and caught. As the group develops greater proficiency, more sock-balls are added. Other variations might also be introduced. For example, a player might wish to introduce a sock-ball that is to be thrown in the reverse direction so that one throws that sock-ball to the player from whom one normally receives the other sock-balls. Sock-ball group juggling is a game which lends itself to constant elaboration and variation.

Baseball   So there you are, all ready to play baseball, and the other team doesn't show up. So you've got nine people. How are you going to play baseball with just nine people?

Well, you make smaller teams, that's all. Except that would give each team four and a half people. So, maybe you should make three teams—three on a side. That'd work.

Except, how do you play baseball with three teams?

9-8: A little sockball juggling.

You have to make something up. What else can you do? So, you put two teams in the field and one team up to bat. And then, after that team's finished batting, one of the other two teams goes up to bat, and you all just take turns. No problem.

But what do you do when bases are loaded? If you've only got three people on a team, what do you do when everybody's on base and there's no one left to pitch to? Well, what you do is call in the other team.

So who gets the points for a run? Well, both teams, naturally. It'll even out, eventually. People will deserve the points they get.

And then you discover that you don't have enough people for the field. Well, don't worry, you'll get them as soon as they make it to the home plate.

Except that now nobody can tell what team anybody's playing for. There you are on Team Two, playing the field with half of Team One. Well, almost half. So, whose team are you on? No problem. You're whatever team you're playing on. After all, it's still baseball, isn't it?

Except that you forgot the bats. You forgot the bats? How could you forget the bats for a baseball game? Oh, the other team was supposed to bring them.

No problem. You just play without bats, that's all.

9-9: Tree baseball—here's the pitch.

9-10: Tree baseball—home safe.

How? Well, let's see, are there any sticks around? No. All right. So, the pitcher throws and the batter catches, that's all. And then the batter throws the ball into the field and runs. Simple, no?

Not that simple. Well, look, we'll make home plate really wide, see, and as long as the pitcher can make the ball cross the base, it's fair, and if the batter can't catch it, it's a strike. And, if she does catch it, she has to throw right away. Throwing's too hard? All right, she has to roll the ball.

But, you don't have a baseball, do you? All you can find is an old playground ball—one of those inflatable red ones.

Perfect. Now you can play kickball, which is really even more like baseball. The pitcher rolls the ball and the batter kicks it. Simple?

All right, so your ball's half out of air. So you throw it and the batter has to hit it with his hand or something—all right, with his shoe. But he can put his shoe on his hand, maybe, so it's easier to hit hard.

So what if the batter's only four years old? You can move the pitcher's mound, can't you? If you get close enough, and throw gently enough, he'll get it. Look, does it really matter what team he's on? He wants to play, doesn't he? You want to play with him, don't you?

All right, the pitcher's blind. No problem. No problem at all. You just get someone behind the plate to call signals to her. Let her practice a few, just to get the feel. Sure, it'll work.

Your first baseman's on a wheelchair? Can he move around fast enough by himself? Does he want someone to push him?

So it isn't a regulation baseball field. So it's a backyard. So it's a small backyard with a tree in the middle.

So, you can always run around the tree, you know. Actually, seeing as the yard's as small as it is, maybe a player has to run around the tree once before he can run to a base.

Well, of course you can still play even though it's raining. Maybe you'd want to take off your shoes so you wouldn't slip so much when you run. Maybe you'd all want to get into your bathing suits. What is more glorious than a game of baseball for nine players with a half-deflated playground ball in a small back-yard around a tree on a rainy day?

So, the other team finally showed up. So, you have six people on a team. So you make a few extra bases or you make people run around the tree two times instead of one.

Unless, of course, you're not sure you want to play baseball any more.

There are a lot of games you can play with eighteen people in a small backyard around a tree in the rain, you know.

Well, there's always golf.

Sure, you make one side of the tree the hole, see, and you make the other side the tee, and then you put a can somewhere that the hitter has to knock over before he can shoot for the hole again. Sure, you can use a whole bunch of cans. Or boxes, even.

All right, so you don't have any golf clubs. So what?

The Games Preserve

There are times when it is important to play with the people who are close—family, friends, colleagues, neighbors. There's a certain kind of sharing, of equality that can only be reached through play. In the pursuit of whatever else—making money, making decisions, making do—people get separated into roles. As parent, mate, child, employer, employee, there is a division that seems to be most easily bridged by play. When a family plays well together, each member of the family has the chance to be on equal footing with every other member. By playing together, the family becomes rejuvenated. When roles are again taken on and other necessities faced, the members of the family have a little more in common because they've played together. Though there is a separation, there is also the experience of equality through play.

Actually, doing anything together, as equals, as members of the same team—washing dishes, deciding on salaries, wandering through the desert—brings close people closer. But, of all things to do together, the easiest and the most equalizing is playing games.

Though it is true that you can play anywhere with anything, it seems to help if you have a special place with special things. It's easier to play in a place that is designed for playing.

There are many such places: bowling alleys, tennis courts, pool halls, baseball diamonds, playgrounds, swimming pools, recreation centers. Each of these places provides a special environment, devoted entirely to play.

As abundant as these places are, none of them is designed to respond to the particular need that people have when they want to play—together.

There's only one game to play on a tennis court. If the whole family or community or staff likes to play tennis, and if everybody gets to play with everybody else, equally, then the tennis court is exactly the right environment. It would be wonderful if you could play like that on a tennis court—wonderful, but highly unlikely.

There's the penny arcade or the bowling alley. But playing in them, side by side with people who, politely or not, are ignoring you, doesn't help bring you closer. Even if it's only one person you want to play with, it becomes difficult to play fully in such an alienating environment. It'd be embarrassing if you shouted too loudly or laughed too much. You'd have trouble even getting into a good argument.

Even recreation centers, as useful as they are to a community, don't seem to be built in such a way as to provide a space where the whole community can play together. The teen lounge, the game room, the senior citizens' room, are all behind closed doors, separate and separating.

There are outdoor spaces to which we can bring materials and people. City and state parks are good places because they offer a general, natural environment that we can explore and define together. Most of the alternative forms of recreation take place there. But, parks are not as accessible as bowling alleys. It requires a greater effort to arrange for a picnic or a trip than it does to go to a community center.

Another kind of space is needed—a space we can design together, like what we do in a park, but more accessible, more capable of responding to the various needs of the people with whom we want to play.

Since we are the designers of this playspace, we can be more certain that it will contain those things that we can play with together. If we are looking for a space for our family, it can be anywhere—in the living room, kitchen, wherever it is easy for us to gather. For more people, we need a larger space.

We design the space by finding out what we like to play with and making sure that we have the materials we need. It's easiest to start with games.

If it's an indoor space, we need indoor games. A deck of cards, a set of checkers, whatever. We'd need enough games so that there would be at least one game that everyone would want to play with. If there are a lot of us, even though we might not all be playing the same game, we would be playing in the same area. We could switch games now and then, and people. So that, sooner or later, everyone had a chance to play with everyone else.

Let's call this space a *"games preserve."* We stock it with as many different kinds of games as we can—games that take mental skills, physical skills, games that require competition or cooperation, puzzles, whatever. The more choices we provide each other, the more guarantees we have that we will be able to find the games we want to play together.

A games preserve can be built anywhere. It can start small. If it's to be a place that serves only the family, it can all be located in a bookshelf. If we want to make it into a space for the community, maybe we need a garage.

We begin by gathering games from our friends. The simplest way to start is by having a games night. We set up as many games as we think will be needed—making sure the pieces are all there and that there is enough space to play each of them. We invite people to bring more games, and food, perhaps, to share. A games night, as informal as it is, is a genuine alternative. It allows people to play together. Children with adults, everybody with anybody. It might be useful to clear a space for some more active games, like charades. It also helps to use the floor for some games and tables for some others.

Whether it is a games night for the family or for the community, as it becomes a regular event, the games preserve enlarges. More games are brought in. Others are taken away. After a while, a facility is created where a games night can happen anytime for anyone who wants to come and play.

An institutional games preserve might need to offer yet more alternatives—a pool table, a ping-pong table, flying rings, an exercise bar, whatever. As you develop a games preserve to serve a wider population, you naturally increase the kinds of games you have to offer. The result is that people who want to play on the flying rings can play side by side with those who want to play checkers. Everybody can play. There's a game for all needs. No one is separated because of what he or she likes to play with. Everybody's together.

The whole staff or community should be involved in designing their games preserve. The more people involved, the more the games preserve serves. In the institution or industry, the games preserve provides everyone, staff as well as clients, with the opportunity to play together. The games preserve becomes a place where we can set aside the divisions between us and the pressures to succeed. We can find another way of being together—one that gives us the chance to meet as equals. If we compete too much during our working time, we can play something silly and cooperative. If we have to work too closely together, we can play something serious and competitive. The games preserve can allow us to restore the balance we need in order to work better together.

A games preserve in a hospital would be different from that in a school or a community. But, in each environment, since it is being designed by the people who want to use it, the games preserve serves to provide equal access to play. As games preserves proliferate, groups can exchange games, widening their libraries and sharing in each other's support.

A games preserve is yet one more alternative. By having different kinds of games preserves, in the country, in the community, in the home, we provide more opportunity to meet the need to play. Any place we can set aside for playing in is the place to start.

A Town of Players

You're in a part of the park that you've never really spent any time in before. You're there with maybe two thousand other people with whom you've never really spent any time before. There's one of your teachers over there. And there's some people with tattoos and earrings. And over there are some children that appear to be brain damaged. And over there's the captain of the basketball team.

And everybody's playing. Except for those who are eating or making food or listening to music or just wandering. On the other hand, they're playing, too, somehow. They're relaxed, easy, smiling a lot.

And it's in living color. In playing color! Green bright grass and grass-streaked sneaker white. Crystal sky and the clash of all the colors of clothes. Moving. Changing. In the brightness of eyes.

Sound. A hundred conversations. Wind. A drift of guitar singing. Laughter. So much laughter!

And you hear:

"Proui? Proui? Proui?"   "Cows over on that side."   "Hi"
"Can she play, too?"   "Dho-dho-dho-dho-dho"   "Can I play?"
"That looks like fun!"   "Say what's this game?"   "She got me!"

Little kids playing with gentle big people. All kinds of people trying to sit on each other's lap. Rows of people passing people overhead, catching people when they fall. Caring. Enjoying.

This is a New Games Tournament—a smørgasbord of approaches to play: people making up rules as they go along—playing with a parachute, a six-foot diameter "earth ball"; people fencing with styrofoam swords; people painting; people dancing; singing. It's all there. Checkers and capture the flag. Rugby and rock dancing.

Everything you ever thought was good about play, every reason you've ever had for wanting to share play, is right here, validated, obvious, accessible to a whole town of people.

That's what it is—a small town. It's an entire human environment—a whole community of communities—playing, experiencing its wholeness.

9-11: A game of stand up.

9-12: The tap game—winning together.

9-13: Instant boundaries.

9-14: People pass.

The New Games Foundation is located in San Francisco. Their address is P.O. Box 7901, San Francisco, California 94120, (415) T.A.G.M.Y. double ZERO.

Since 1974, when the foundation was begun by Pat Farrington, they have been working, struggling, playing to bring New Games Tournaments to the places where there are people who want to play—everywhere.

It was the first New Games Tournament, organized by Stewart Brand, editor of the Whole Earth Catalog, that led to the creation of the foundation. Since then, this group of people has developed training programs to help people put together their own New Games Tournaments, films, slide-tapes, a newsletter to keep people in touch, a network to help people find each other, programs designed to be used in schools, hospitals, parks and recreation centers. They have grown this capable because of sheer dedication of people like Burton Naiditch and John O'Connell and of whatever support they have been able to find—donations, selling "earth balls," whatever.

And all their efforts have made wonderful things come to pass.

chapter 10

The Ball

by James C. McCullagh

In the town of Fairfield, Connecticut, is a field where giants of the afternoon can do battle without sporting huge biceps or suffering familiar football bruises.

A place for the kids to come. And the middle-aged. The young and old.

It is an experiment station. A grassy field. A field of praise.

It is the site of an invention: a two-decade pursuit of a universal game, which would be as acceptable to the Chinese as to the West. To the boy and the girl, the man and the woman.

A game for all seasons. A game of cooperation. A game that doesn't stop. A game where there are no spectators. A game where everyone plays. A game based on the uncanny logic of kids: that whatever moves is fun, whatever keeps moving is more fun.

A game that evolved from the heart and mind of a family man, Judge John Henry Norton.

The Evolution

Judge Norton, who has fourteen children (including five adopted orphans), labored for nearly two decades to find a sport that would be agreeable to all age groups under all sorts of circumstances.

Because he believes that children get "out of" play and into rigid sports too early, he looked, and thought, and spent years experimenting. Different balls, different bats, different games, dif-

239

ferent techniques, different people—looking for the right combination. The criteria he was trying to satisfy were fairly simple:

> He wanted a game that everyone could play.
> He wanted a game that was easy to play.
> He wanted a game that would cut across age barriers.
> He wanted a game that was continuous.
> He wanted a game that could be played on the playground or outside of retirement homes.
> He wanted a game in which the full body would play.
> He wanted a game that evolved from activities people were familiar with.
> He wanted a game the kids wanted.
> He wanted a game that encouraged ingenuity.
> He wanted a game that was truly recreational.
> He wanted a lifesport.
> He wanted a game that people had been waiting for.
> He got hocker.

"We began," he reports, "with a variation of soccer. But many of the children found it too confining. They liked to use their hands and they didn't like the continual delays from out-of-bounds and other interruptions created by too many whistles. Gradually, over seventeen years, the present game evolved, with the form of the sport determined by experience on the field. By last year, the enthusiastic reactions of both small kids and of athletic friends in their twenties convinced me that the sport was at a point where the whole country could play it. Families, superstars, team members, kids on the corner lot—everybody could get in on the action."

Norton, a child of athletic scholarships, has no ax to grind against traditional sports. "However," he remarks, "traditional team sports simply do not meet today's requirements. In addition to being a budgetary burden, they involve too few people and, in many cases, even those winning a varsity letter are losing out when it comes to health benefits.

"Probably the most fascinating feature of hocker is that anyone can play it. Novices and handicapped persons play it because they will never be embarrassed playing the sport. If the ball happens to come to them, they will manage to get some part of their body on the ball. There is instant success. The unathletic person

10-1: Judge John Henry Norton.

10-2: Men and women can play this game on equal terms.

can play on the same team with superior athletes and not look foolish at all. It's an amazing thing.

"Hocker is also a marvelous 'family picnic sport' as well. Grandparents can play it with their grandchildren."

The Game

In Norton's words, hocker is a grass roots "game that cares about the people who play it. It cares about developing, not hurting, their bodies so that its rules preclude violence. It cares about not hurting their *feelings* so no one playing informally even has to stand on the sidelines for want of size or skill."

There are no sidelines at the Norton house when a hocker game is under way. Just people, balls, and feeling, as family and neighborhood turn out for a game.

The hocker field dips down from the house like a suburban plain. The field, approximately sixty yards long by thirty yards wide, sports unfamiliar goalposts at either end. There are rectangles and squares to receive the ball. The ball, too large to be palmed by a massive hand, is simply a hocker globe, risen to a tubular roundness to incite pleasure.

Judge Norton does not make any formal announcement. The men and women, kids and adults, come in dribs and drabs, as if called by the unsung king of sport. At 1:30 sharp, or thereabouts, they crawl up the avenue, the hocker walk as they call it. They come in spite of the ninety-five-degree heat or the twenty-degree cold.

They come although some walk with difficulty. They come although some of them cannot speak English. They come from New York, New Jersey, Massachusetts, and from around the town.

Football players have heard this is a good way to stay in shape for the fall. Some middle-aged people have learned this is a good way to have recreational fun without getting hurt. So they come.

Their first stop is the ball, which is easy to conquer. Rather, the ball conquers you. You sense you have to do something with it. You lean against it, kick it, jump on it, bounce on it, dribble it, elbow it, knee it, shoulder it, everything but carry it in your hands.

Some players will proceed like a ballerina down the field bouncing the ball off their palms as if it were a hotcake (this is

10-3: You can kick the ball, as in soccer.

called currying). Some, born to basketball, will dribble with this whale of a ball down the length of the hocker court. Others will mercifully try to dribble this oversized soccer ball to the cavern of the goal. Others will simply pass it, move it, shove it, bounce it, shoot it, with any part of their body that's convenient. One handicapped boy who could not move well found a way to move the ball very well. It was a globe he could contend with. Not the impeccable baseball, the missile of a pigskin, the dot of a soccer ball, or the invisible tennis ball. The hocker ball was something he could grab. A mass not likely to be forgotten or neglected during the run of the game.

Judge Norton separates the teams by lots, according to age and weight. He sweeps two teams into his net and the reds and yellows (for they must don jerseys) go down to the field where the big ball waits.

There are rules, ways to play the game, things to do and not to do, approaches and techniques, points of order and recommendations. But you really need none of this at first; you are thrown on the field with a ball and you play. Any kid from Mexico, Newark, or Timbuktu can be dropped on the field and will know what to do with the ball. It's as easy as that. And the adult can

10-4: You can dribble the ball, as in basketball.

10-5: This is called "currying" the ball.

walk on the field and move the hocker ball. There are no pep talks, no rallies, no huddles. Even the referee plays the game. That's one of the rules. No professional referees in this game.

And what do you need to know to begin the game? Only one thing really: you can't carry the ball. No, not even the goalie. Everyone is equal. And only in the hocker face-off circle do you use your feet exclusively. Otherwise, your whole body plays.

The game moves like an uncertain flood. Since no one really plays any set positions, you do not find tidy pockets of people standing around as you would in a soccer game. In hocker, humanity will surge, chasing that bouncing beach ball—like madcap kids on the green. The beauty of it is that you can always get something on the ball. If you can't hit it with your hands, hit it with your head, your knee, your foot, your elbow; anything, just to keep it moving. And that's exactly what people do.

The game can be played at its own intensity, depending on the energies of those participating. But whether it's kids or adults playing, the game is continuous; it is not stopped for throw-ins or apologies. The game follows the ball.

And no one can pounce on the ball, bringing the game to a halt. Movement is continuous; the game doesn't stop. It does not even stop at one of the goals. Since the game continues beyond and behind the goals, the hocker ball is a double threat, a double agent of exhaustion.

And no goalie can lay his final hands on the ball, bringing the game to rest. He is no better or worse than any other player; he must play by the rules of continuous motion.

The unexpected is always likely to happen in this game. You never really own the ball; you cannot hold it in your hand. Actually, the ball is always free of you, floating either off your foot, your hand, your elbow, your legs. And since the ball is so big, it is very easy for a foot, an elbow, an arm or leg from the opposing team to get in the way.

No one owns the turf in this game. There are no yard markers, no hash marks. The game is designed to be played on a continuous city lot.

There seems no killer urge in this game. On the contrary, players take the time out to cheer the moves of their opponents. Certainly there is an urge to win, but not at the expense of others. No one appears to trample over others in this sport.

10-6: The hocker ball is light and easily passed.

So hocker is not bloodthirsty; and one even senses a good bit of cooperation. The "well done" you hear on the court is not an echo from an English cricket match but a commentary on the lively art of hocker, the game where people don't forget that they are people, the game where people playing the game can even stay related.

Perhaps most of all hocker refreshes our memory of play. Perhaps it reminds us that the center of sport should be continuous play, where age can indeed be the child in a man.

Perhaps the real test of a universal game is that anyone can play it; that it cuts across age and cultural barriers the positive way. Evidence of this universality was captured by the score of native Mexican children who fell onto the field in disarray and within minutes had mastered the game sufficiently to make the ball jump.

Another aspect of the universality of the game is that there are no spectators; anyone on the sidelines is actually waiting for his turn to begin. In this respect, hocker is like the brand of soccer in which everyone must play.

Still another aspect of the universality of the game is that there seems to be a built-in cooperativeness in the players, spontaneous cheering of good plays and points; a reluctance to break ankles; an opportunity for the nondescript, the backbencher.

Norton's dream is cosmopolitan. He sees hocker filling the beaches and playgrounds, the schools and clubs, the lots outside of retirement homes. He sees a generation of children growing with a sport that they can stay with throughout their lives and, unlike other popular American pastimes, can actually pass along to their children as a kind of cultural sports gift which his generation did not collect.

Oddly enough, there appears to be little fouling taking place in the game or, perhaps more accurately, fewer opportunities to foul, or a diminished desire to foul, possibly, because the game does not consist of start, lunge, and stop.

And, medically speaking, you play the game with your lungs as well as your hands: hocker is aerobic; you get all the running that you need. In fact, it is not uncommon for the veteran hocker players to ask the newcomers whether the running was sufficient, a kind of inside joke inaugurated by those who are defensive about the game, by those who do not want to underestimate the physical exertion demanded by the sport.

The Play

Two teams, each with nine members divided among males and females, oppose each other on a rectangular field one hundred yards long and sixty yards wide surrounded by a four-foot-high fence. Play is virtually continuous with no time-outs, no off-sides and few whistles. Action between the teams surges back and forth between goalposts which have distinctive double crossbars forming two rectangles with a square in the middle.

A lanky orange player dribbles the jumbo-sized (sixteen-inch diameter) rubber ball up the field, expertly faking his way past a burly white defender who tries unsuccessfully to upset his balance with a one-handed push at shoulder level. The orange player spots a teammate near the white goal and kicks to him on the run. But a diminutive, speedy white player intercepts.

She slaps the ball down to control it but is careful not to hold it in her hand, a violation. She runs toward midfield, bouncing the ball in the palm of her hand so that it is continuously in motion. The white attacker sees the opportunity for a bounce

10-7: The hocker goal.

pass to a teammate streaking toward the orange goal.

The pass misses and caroms off the fence behind the goal. But an alert white player catches up to the carom and, from a point *behind* the goal, kicks it. The ball sails through one of the rectangles formed by the double crossbars and the referee raises the kicker's hand and blows his whistle, signaling four points.

The play ultimately is the thing. Seven points wins a set, and two out of three or four out of seven sets wins a match. There are no time limits. Goalposts are fifteen feet high and eighteen feet apart. The lower crossbar is nine feet above ground level, the upper, twelve feet. In the middle between the crossbars is a yard-square target with rectangles formed by the crossbars and posts on either side. All points above the lower crossbar must be kicked in; points below it may be kicked, punched, slapped or otherwise propelled by any part of the body.

Points may be scored from either side of the goalposts. A kick above the top crossbar scores one point, through the rectangles four points and through the interior square, five points. Everything scored under the lower crossbar scores three points with the exception of the penalty kick scoring two points. Penalty kicks are made from ten yards out with two defenders permitted in the goal.

Teams are comprised of a blocker whose primary duty is to guard the goal, two defensive ends, two offensive ends and two wings who normally range on offense and defense. Finally, there are two "free agents" who are basic playmakers and who direct the flow of play. However, no team member including the blocker is prohibited from entering any portion of the field at any time, and field markings represent general areas of responsibility and are tactical aids rather than lines which can mark off-side zones as in football or hockey. Thus, there are no off-sides, and blockers may be assisted in the goal mouth by any number of their teammates.

Hocker operates with the least number of rules consistent with orderly, non-violent play. Its cardinal rule forbids picking up or holding the ball in one or both hands. It must remain in continuous motion although a move called "currying" permits a player to advance while bouncing the ball from hand to hand or juggling it in one hand like a hot potato. The ball may be kicked, dribbled, bounce-passed, punched, slapped, scooped or head-butted.

Games and play action following scores begin with a "square-off" in a midfield circle where two opposing free agents place their insteps against the ball and kick it away at the referee's signal.

Penalty shots are awarded for a variety of offenses including illegal pushing (above the shoulders), blocking, tackling, tripping, or deliberate rough play which is decided at the referee's discretion. Infractions such as picking up the ball and holding it result in a "take-off" or free pass by the opposing team from the point of infraction. Take-offs similarly are used after a ball is propelled over the four-foot-high enclosure.

The Rules

The game starts with a square-off in midfield. There are no time-outs, no off-sides and only balls over the fence are out-of-bounds. Balls kicked or punched out-of-bounds, or other minor violations, bring a take-off for the other team, that is, a free chance to put the ball back into play.

You Can . . .

Slap, curry, basketball dribble, soccer dribble, kick, punch, push or slap-pass the ball, with two hands or one.

Scoop up the ball with one hand.

Male versus male can push anybody with one hand shoulder level to waist level in ball pursuit.

Females can push males with two hands, other females with one hand.

Passively block (basketball type).

All soccer moves except a "soccer tackle" *from behind.*

Curry at head level or below.

"Shoulder bump" only in pursuit of the ball. (*Not* football shoulder block.)

Score from either side of goalposts.

"Hold your ground" and an offensive player must avoid you.

Slight, incidental body contact is okay.

Kick a three-point goal from the take-off position.

Score by hand under first crossbar.

You Cannot . . .

Major Penalties:

"Football tackle," "football block," hold or charge.

Push with two hands.

Push anybody above shoulder levels or below waists.
"Soccer tackle" from behind.
Males cannot push females.

Minor Penalties:

Scoop up the ball with two hands.
Pick up, hold, or carry ball.
Throw the ball above your shoulder level.
Curry above head level.

You cannot kick one, four or five points from the take-off position. (If ball goes in these areas, there is no score, but the ball remains in play.)

Penalty shots score two points. Seven points wins a set, two of three sets or three of five or four of seven sets wins the match.

Penalties:

Major: Direct kick on goal from exactly ten yards out. Two defenders. Players line up on triangle. Defenders must have both feet on white goal line.

Minor: All other penalties are minor. The offender gives up possession and the closest opposition player has a take-off. On a take-off, the opposition must give a five-yard radius. The offensive player can do anything with the ball at this point, according to the rules.

The "O-Zones": In the formal game, the circles near the goal are called O-Zones. Any penalty incurred here is serious. A "major" violation means two direct kicks on goal; with a "minor" violation, there is one direct kick on goal (instead of the usual take-off).

In informal hocker, you can improvise with the goalposts. One point over a crossbar, three points under. The fascinating quintuple-zone goalposts can come later. Use a fenced-in area if you can for exciting caroms. Have as little out-of-bounds as possible that is consistent with safe play. Supervisor should use judgement on pushing if there is disparity in ages, strength, etc.

The Beginning

According to Judge Norton, you can get started with very little equipment. A sixteen-inch playground ball will do. In the beginning, soccer or football goalposts can be used. "We have often used," Norton reports, "trash cans as goalposts." If the ball goes over the imaginary line along the top of the trash cans, then one point is scored (and these must be scored by foot, of course). If the ball goes below the imaginary line, then three points are scored. Or you may want to determine the imaginary crossbar line by taking the average height of the players involved.

Participants have found that sixty yards between goalposts is ideal with nine players. If you have more than sixty yards, then put more players on each team. But if you have "better" players on one team, you might want more players on the other. Improvise, experiment, invent.

The important thing is that you play—together.

After that, if you want to learn more about the game, write to Sports Tigers, P.O. Box 768, 54 Miller Street, Fairfield, Connecticut 06430.

chapter 11

The Run

by James C. McCullagh

What's in the run? Why should we consider the run a natural horse movement? A dance? A chance for us to walk on water?

Go to the playground and watch the children run. They don't really run; they lope like antelope and the description is correct. They move, they frolic, they leap; they stop and they go. They run backwards, shunting like a train in reverse. They run forward in many special gears. They move sideways in dancer's

11-1

11-2

11-1 through 11-3:
Frank White: Runner.

11-3

step. They move in the large white round of the circle. They move as if their spines were rubber.

They are indeed elastic creatures.

But as the saying goes: Time creeps on like a restless tide and before too long we are moving in squares and rectangles, pyramids of muscle. Blocks of strength.

We're moving to the cadence of wood. And no more long chases after nothing.

No longer the rush to catch the bus. Not that embarrassment. In fact, running amidst walking people is a real embarrassment, as George Leonard points out in his book, *The Ultimate Athlete*. Leonard recounts the time when, like a gazelle, he was racing through the streets of New York. Gradually he noticed that the walkers and those riding in buses were interested in his movement; in fact, they seemed to give him the dead-eye stare, entreating him to slow down, silently accusing this moving human of doing something wrong in traffic. Of moving too fast for conditions. Of using his legs when he could have used the bus.

Leonard sensed in the sullenness of the crowd a conspiracy, a collective attempt to slow him down, an effort to stop his running. For isn't the runner, in a world that does not move, a strange and forbidding creature? Isn't he the foreigner in jogging shoes? Isn't he that flash of youthful lightning people want to forget, to hide from under a protective tree?

So perhaps people run to be playful, to be like little children, to keep them in shape to chase the bus. Perhaps some people do it to get attention. Take the case of Frank White of Whippany, New Jersey, who reports, "About four years ago I started a new job at a plant located in Murry Hill, New Jersey. Initially, I was placed in a small office which seemed to receive the full blast of the air conditioning. Although it was midsummer and the outside temperatures were ranging into the nineties, I was just freezing in that office.

"Even wearing my suit jacket didn't seem to help, so when lunch-time came I just had to go outside into the heat of the day to 'thaw out.' I would take a short walk and use up most of my forty-five minutes just walking the neighborhood. I began to enjoy the walks and when wintertime came and it got quite cold, I decided it might be good to just jog along for a while! Well, I am long gone out of that small office and now every day use my whole lunch period just jogging the Murry Hill area. At first I felt strange because I'm always attired in dress shirt, tie, and sport jacket. I thought—perhaps people will just think that this old man (I am forty-six years old with gray hair) is late for lunch. Now I don't really care, but I do still get stopped occasionally by a policeman ("What's the problem?") or by someone wanting to give me a lift!"

And is to run to be born or reborn? One sixty-year-old man from Quebec, who jogs ten miles every morning at a six- to seven-mile-an-hour clip, ended a letter this way, "It may sound trite or perhaps boastful to say this, but I could not terminate this short account on myself without mentioning that I feel somewhat reborn both physically and mentally. It's as simple as that.

"I feel grateful to my Maker for making it possible for the body and mind to sort of regenerate themselves through effort and obedience to his natural laws. To one being 'reborn' it becomes so clear that the body and its vitality cannot be maintained in its created integrity with little or no activity."

And to Kathy Schutt from Boston, "jogging is a love-hate relationship which, at its worst, is sluggish and uncomfortable. At its best, however, as I slip into my subconsciousness and rhythm, it is ecstasy, a universal communion, a sense of timelessness, a joyous flight, a spiritual gift, a perfect union of mind, body, and spirit. Being a nurse I know the benefits of collateral coronary circulation, the importance of aerobic endurance, and the aesthetics of tight, well-defined musculature. I run for these reasons in the beginning. But when I "let go," the joy of my body's movement becomes effortless, energizing, and blending with all that is. I run to catch those moments which just happen by doing it and by being there. Perhaps running is transformation."

Phyllis Tennant of Severna Park, Maryland, believes in transformation. "My story," she reports, "began five years and fifty pounds ago. When I first met my husband, he was into a physical fitness routine centered largely around running, and I had no physical activity inclination whatsoever. With our wedding date six months away, he very lovingly suggested that I lose some weight and get into better shape. So, I thought that that was a reasonable request and decided to join him in running. The first day I ran about an eighth of a mile and collapsed with nauseating fatigue. This really angered me to think I was twenty-one and already in such degenerative condition.

"From that day forward began my battle with myself. As I continued to diet, I continued to try to increase my running. Finally by my wedding day, I had lost forty pounds and could run

11-4

11-4 & 11-5.
Kathy Schutt: Runner.

11-5

a mile regularly. After marriage came the challenge to keep the weight off; I was determined. So, I made exercise my morning cup of coffee. Each day I arose before my husband, did my penance, returned to shower and dress with vigor for my day.

"Gradually, exercise changed my mind as well as my body. It is an exercise in mental discipline as well as physical. Because it is never easy, this makes the pride of accomplishment even more sweet. Running is my time of the day; the world is fresh and waking to a new day. My ninety-pound German shepherd now accompanies me through our neighborhood on our 6:00 a.m., three-mile run. Now I could never stop, for the neighbors would all wonder where their alarm clock is!

"Lots of people ask for my formula, especially people who knew the old me. They are totally baffled by the new me. I tell them it is a matter of the mind, i.e., mind over matter. One must want to do something so much that no other obstacle is going to stop them. For example, I ran in twelve inches of snow in twenty-eight degrees below zero in Ohio. I ran until I was six weeks away from delivering my daughter who, by the way, was born in one-half hour because of my conditioning. The day after delivery I weighed the same as before pregnancy.

"Not only am I hooked on my morning run, but my dog is also! He also actually cries until I come get him to go with me. Both of us run side by side breathing the dewy air, watching the squirrels scamper after their breakfast, and listening to the birds chatter. We seldom see anyone else; if they are along the way, we do not even notice. I return home with some problem resolved, some new tidbit of nature observed with heart pumping vigorously and legs aching. I wouldn't have it any other way."

Phyllis Tennant has clearly been transformed. She has taken the run, or rather the run has taken her, far beyond the stretching of muscles on a linear plane. It has taken her to birth, to the very center of her life. Psychologically, she has been transformed; when running she sees nothing else, not the time of day, not the man next door. She runs and proceeds in a narrow range of ecstasy, allowing her wall to move effortlessly before her.

That is a transformation.

What surprises some people is that running is indeed play, perhaps a playing back to childhood. Some people discover later in life that running can return us to our natural state. Roland B.

Hawkins of Beaufort, North Carolina, discovered that. His story:

"I'm thirty-four and very married, have a steady job, home is paid for, and I still love my wife, looking for another car and best of all I believe in God. Guess you would call me an average man that leads a pretty average life. Except for one thing, I'm a dedicated jogger. I live it, I believe in it. I do it in the rain, in the snow, in the cold, and at night. With me it has become a daily ritual that I look forward to. I need it like a junkie needs 'horse.' I dream about it. It has become a part of my life like air and water. Jogging is where it is at.

"All this wasn't so about a year and a half ago. I was an over-weight slob that dreamed about food, cigarettes, and television. In that order. All I did was look over the bank of the rut I was in to see how the world was doing and then I was back at it again. The transition took place just before January 1, 1976, when I took a good long look at myself and got to thinking. I had been pretty slim and trim all my life, now I was a 165-pound blimp. When I was a kid I could run like a deer and easily turned a 10.2 in the hundred yard dash back in 1959. When I was in the Marines, I did plenty of running and even went out for the Division Track Team for a while. So why was I suddenly a grease ball?

"Okay, so on January 1, 1976, I started doing a few exercises and I gave up tobacco. Man, it was cold turkey but I stuck with it. I started trotting the streets a little, too. In about a month or so I got hold of the YMCA book on physical fitness. I went through their five-month exercise plan. I was really getting geared up then and the fat was melting away. I was counting calories during this time also. Well, after the five-month thing I started the challenge in jogging offered by the President's Council on Physical Fitness. Now I was on the road and I mean the road. I was sweating and puffing. Sweat dripping off my nose and forehead and burning my eyes. All through this I was discovering something. I could still run like a deer and I loved it."

Perhaps the essence of running is play, a state of mind which allows us to be mindful of the playful world around us. Jack K. Holcomb of Laureldale, Pennsylvania, claims that "running is an escape for me. I use this 'outlet' to keep the cobwebs from over-taking my mind, to maintain good physical condition and to enjoy the countryside. I even suppose that running is a kind of TM

11-6

11-7

11-6 & 11-7: Phyllis Tennant: Runner.

practice for me. If there are any pressing problems that must be dealt with I seem to handle them better after mulling them over 'on the road.'

"I'm also an avid birdwatcher and can take the time to watch and/or listen as I travel through a wooded glade. Running also presents the opportunity to commune with other facets of nature that give me great peace. Whether it's a quick glance of a field of daisies or the observation of a butterfly in flight. To sum it all up, if that is possible, there is a peacefulness in running that can't be found anywhere else in my life. Perhaps the tranquility combined with the physical exertion that offers all of these benefits to my soul gives me a peace of mind that I need to cope with the 'every-day'."

Running is play, sidestepping to enthusiasm. James J. Johnson of Iowa City, Iowa, reports that he "did not learn how to run until I was nearly unable to walk.

"After my teenage years, my life slowed down to a crawl; I would walk at no opportunity. Nothing could get me going. Kids would whiz by me and I would think to myself that that isn't going to last very long; they will soon get tired and realize that running ends with an early age.

"This I was convinced of.

"But when I stopped chasing after buses, when I stopped running across the street, or after the dog, strange and subtle things happened. I also gave up stair climbing. I lost my fervor for life. Anything was too much trouble.

"The result was that I collected weight around my waist and arms like ringlets. I couldn't even run after my children. In fact, I had trouble putting two strong steps together.

"The more the world went by, the more I sat; the slower I became.

"By the time I was forty, I knew I had to do something; I knew I had to discover my legs. I knew I had to pull a couple of steps together. And this I tried.

"It was slow going, like learning to crawl all over again. The walk to the store was a physical chore. The walk to town was drudgery. But I kept doing it until I could do it, until I could pick up the pace, until I could walk quickly, and once, to my complete surprise, on the main street of town, I broke into a slow-as-water jog. I don't know why; I just wanted to move faster than I was going, which really wasn't very fast at all. Perhaps I wanted to move faster than the man in front of me. Perhaps I really wanted to show him my heels. Actually, I don't think any of these were the real reasons. I'm sure the ground or perhaps my body was telling me that I really could move faster than I was, that there was some spring in my step, that all hope was not lost.

"No, I didn't go right into jogging; in truth, I didn't go jogging at all. I was too satisfied, too content with my quick step and that I stayed with and improved upon. Now as I walk to the store I will occasionally do so backwards or perhaps run backwards for a few steps or perhaps stutter-step to the side like a boxer. Or perhaps I will do the hop, step and jump or maybe dash for twenty or thirty yards, or run in circles or jump up and down like a ball. Or do crazy military maneuvers as I walk down the sidewalk, raising my knees up so high that they feel like they are touching my chin. Or sometimes I will stop and enjoy a tumble on a neighbor's lawn.

"People have ceased to be amazed at what I do; actually, I think, because it is not really amazing after all. If I feel like I want to hop, skip and jump then I hop, skip and jump. The kids do the same thing and sometimes even mimic me, which is not really true because actually I'm mimicking them. Or sometimes we join together and go hopping, skipping and jumping down the street in spite of all the raised eyebrows.

"I have no intention of running crazy in a straight line, as if I'm really anxious to get from A to B. And I'm not going to run around an oval track like I'm stuck on the end of a string. And I don't want to run up sand dunes or run through a forest with a flag in my pocket.

"No, all I really want to do is play. I want to be able to do all those crazy twists and turns that kids do. That is enough. How can anyone ask for a better game. I know I can't. 'Cause I've learned to walk again."

Possibly only someone who has come near to experiencing not walking can appreciate the play of the run. Mr. R. G. Waltenbaugh of North Apollo, Pennsylvania, says this about what motivated him to run: "Perhaps one motivation is that at the age of nine or ten I had polio which, while not paralyzing me, did leave me so weak that I could not walk across the floor. In the back of my mind I remember that, and while it took me a few years to find that jogging was an activity I enjoyed, I have found it."

There appears to be a certain loneliness in the game that

runners enjoy. According to Frank L. Goldcamp of Schwenks-ville, Pennsylvania, "I love all sports but I have found frustration in team sports where you must depend on the conditioning and skills of your teammates. In running, your failures or successes directly reflect your own efforts. There are no bad bounces or poor officiating. There is only the pure sport. One foot in front of the other. The first one there wins. That is simplicity at its best. Also with running you can do it anywhere at any time in any weather. It is wonderful therapy for whatever ails me. If I'm angry, running dissipates the anger. If I'm depressed, running lifts my spirits."

Some people are sure that running cultivates a playful trance. "I was doing my jogging," reports Mary Patch of Washington, D.C., "á la Marcel Marceau—that is to say, measured, loosely, very slowly, since I'm on my way to sixty-seven—who wants to go any faster—through our National Zoo here in D.C. at 6 in the morning. The all-night policeman called out: 'There's an animal loose!'

"Steady on. No change in my speed, I responded with, 'Oh? What kind?'

" 'A cheetah!'

"Still no change in my pace and speed.

"The policeman was not kidding. Two of them trotted up a tree trunk felled by the high winds of the previous night.

"Up to this time I wondered about joggers. They look as though they are in a trance. It is apparent I've achieved the same level."

As with other types of play, running can enable us to return to a primitive, natural state, where we are at one with our sur-roundings. Consider the account about "blind jogging" by Bill Gordon.

"We are jogging along Pacific Beach (on the ocean in San Diego, California) when Dyverke Spino, Esalen's physical fitness coach, says, 'Now, make soft eyes.' This, she explains, means letting the eyelids relax and nearly close. One can still see through the slits, but the scene suddenly becomes one of softness and restfulness, and lacks strong definition. Nice and easy. I once read about the tremendous amount of energy required to just see, so it came as no surprise that closing my eyes would really con-serve energy. Just the normal daily activity of 'seeing' drains the body's supply of power.

"One day, I decided to go one step further in the 'soft eyes' approach. If almost closing the eyes could make one feel relaxed—how much better would it be if I could close them all the way?

"One of the advantages of running along the water's edge, in the hard sand, is that with the tide out, the smooth, wide stretch of sand enables one to see—far into the distance—any obstructions that might be on the path of the jogger. You can easily spot seashells or seaweed. Another advantage of the beach is the 'firm-soft' quality of the sand at the water's edge. It's perfect for jogging barefoot and 'gives' the right amount that helps one avoid shin splints and the jarring effect of cement surfaces.

"I picked a place with about a hundred yards of nice, smooth sand stretching out ahead. I went 'soft eyes' and then went all the way. Suddenly, for the first time in my life, I ran with no vision! It was an eerie feeling in the beginning. One of slight fear of where to put my feet and, 'am I veering to the right or left?'

"Every fifty feet or so there was a compulsion to open my eyes a bit and see just where I was stepping. But during those moments of jogging with my eyes closed, I felt an increased sense of awareness of what my entire body was doing; how my head was held, my shoulders, where my feet were—and all those 'proper alignments' that seem so difficult to imagine with the eyes open. I knew I was on to something.

"I invited Art Durson, a blind friend, to go jogging with me on the beach. We used a long, light plastic pole and I led as we took off down the beach. He loved it, and after awhile I got the idea that even without the guiding pole, directions can be given verbally by the sighted person to the other one; such as 'a little to the left' . . . 'steady' . . . 'now a little to the right.'

"A couple of things come out of all this. One is developing an unusual trust in the person who 'guides.' Another is the exalted feeling of turning oneself over completely to the sensations of nature and the new awareness of one's body."

chapter 12

The Quest

by James C. McCullagh

Perhaps we should look at sports and recreation as kind of a quest. A quest for what? Entertainment. Pleasure. Self-fulfillment. Rebirth.

Perhaps sports is a kind of fantasy. A dream of the highest leap; of throwing a Joe Namath aerial; of lasting a round with Ali.

Then again, perhaps it is traditional sport that is fantasy and lifetime recreation which is not.

Men, in their demon youth, have occupied the grass and field. Women have stayed in the shade, content to watch. (Fortunately, this scene is changing).

But what do you do after the teamsport jersey no longer fits? What do you do when televised sports are the only games you enjoy? How do you adjust your new-found leisure time?

Some people, such as Joseph Zweben of Long Island, New York, hang on to traditional games with a frenzy, eager to master the moves of the young. His story:

"Who says you can't teach an old dog new tricks? Well, I say so. I'm age fifty, athletic, and the new trick I'm trying so hard to learn is to play basketball the way the pros do these days in the seventies. I'm a dirty, old player from way back, and the new moves I see at the Garden or on television are making my game obsolete. They play the game clean.

"The pros make it look so easy. Walt Frazier comes down the court with the ball. He's moving in sideways, dribbling one hand to the other, his body protecting the ball. He's so shifty you can't even get a crack at him. He maneuvers behind a block

12-1: Joseph Zweben (left) at play.

set up by a teammate, jumps, hangs in midair, pops with one hand, and zingo, the ball goes in. This is a standard play, no sweat and no defenseman jabs him in the face. I try the same play in the schoolyard and I look like a turkey flying out of a cave. All flutter, and I can't get off the ground smoothly. I keep expecting someone to clobber me.

"First of all, I don't know how to dribble or fake, and I can't even get off a jump shot. Who needed this in my day? All I knew what to do was pivot, or hand off, and fight like a terror under the basket. Elbowing, pushing off, climbing over anyone in my way—this made me a big man. One of the proudest moments of my life was about ten years ago when I ran into an old schoolyard buddy of mine socially, and in front of my wife and kid, he said, 'Yeah, Whitey, I remember you pretty well. You were rough under the boards.'

"That's the whole point. I love the game so much, I give it my best every time out. I don't want to look like a stiff when I'm out there, so I can't take time out to learn the new moves. Oh, if only I could get off one, clean jump shot. If only I could learn to drive, clean.

"Guys my age have given up basketball, but I still feel the same pull whenever I'm in a schoolyard. Of course the guys I play against get younger and younger, and better and better, but I still won't concede and call them kids. Any guy that can dribble by me and I can't even grab his shirt or trip him—that's no kid out there; that's some man.

"These guys I play against today are so damn elusive. I can't elbow. They already have the ball and are off and running before I can shout. If I try to pivot like I did thirty years ago, three guys would block me out so I can't even charge for a tap-in.

"In my day the middle was always crowded, no one dared drive through. A good clip kept them shooting from the outside. That's why there were so many two-handed set shooters. A shooting hand was usually bruised and limp.

"About three years ago something happened on the court which still has me puzzled. This guy I'm guarding pulls a legitimate block on me, and his teammate with the ball is free and clear for the shot. The blocker is firmly standing there, holding his ground. By this time I'm too tired to scoot around him to cut off the shot, so I push him smack into the ball-handler. Of course I knew it was a foul, and I said, 'Okay. It's your out. Your ball.'

They got so mad at me, both of them, one kid finally sputtered, 'But sir, you can't do that on the basketball court.'

"When they start calling me 'sir' I'm ready to change school-yards. Am I getting to look my age? Are they merely tolerating my dirty, old plays? No, in all fairness, what dates me is my old style of play—the hook shots, the pivots, all the running one-handers from the side, I mix them up and keep using them all the time, whichever is fitting that day.

"I still think I play a pretty good game, but I have come to marvel at the ball players of today. The guys I see on TV—their timing, their accuracy, the plays they set up, the ball handling, and their jump shots—boy, do I envy those jump shots! How do they do it? Even dribbling down court on the fast break they could stop on a dime, and up they go suspended in midair. They can hang up there for eternity.

"How are you going to hack a guy like that? Even the guy selling peanuts would spot the foul. But I like to fantasize. If only I could work the ball behind the screen. Not fast, just slow and methodical. If only I could pull a beauty of a head fake, throw my man out of position, and go up as he comes down fouling me, and I pop it in, then complete the three-point play. If only I could pull off one pretty play—you know, it might all have been worth it."

Joe is no spectator in the game of basketball or life. He plays his game with gusto. He understands the grace of the sport and how it eventually leaves most people behind. But Joe continues to throw hook shots against the clock. He is both inside and outside the game. His game stopped thirty years ago but he still plays it, undaunted by the strategies and moves which have purified the sport.

Yet he hangs on doggedly, exhibiting both pleasure and curiosity at the forms that evolved from his mongrel game.

More often than not, people give up participating in traditional sports after high school or college, a move which customarily leaves a large gap in their recreational life.

A question: What is one to do for the next forty or fifty years? Well, there are all sorts of possibilities. All you need is ingenuity. Take Merlin Wessels of Geneva, Illinois, who was at a golf course and invented the following game.

"One hot, humid evening I was walking across a golf course and discovered a golf ball which had apparently been lost. At first

12-2

12-3

12-2 through 12-4: The Quest.

12-4

not thinking much of my find, I thought of possible ways to use the golf ball.

"I finally hit upon the idea of using it to play golf as it was intended. However, one problem existed—I had no golf clubs. To compensate for the lack of clubs I decided to throw the golf ball down the fairways onto the greens counting each throw as an equivalent of a stroke. Once on the greens, the golf ball could be tossed over- or underhand to the hole, or as I prefer, roll the ball like a marble to the hole.

"Plenty of exercise from the game from chasing after the golf ball. A golf course can be quite long with all the zig-zagging you do. In addition to all the exercise one can gain from this game, a person can become quite competitive with traditional golf after some practice. I was able to reach scores in the high thirties for nine holes."

But if ingenuity in recreational activities can be demonstrated on the wide expanses of the golf course, it can also be shown in more private and perhaps primitive ways.

For example, Melanie Zinkham reports that "We often amuse our children and ourselves (especially on long, cold winter nights) by casting hand shadows on the wall. This simple pastime, which probably began in the caves of our remotest ancestors, is still entertaining and at least as stimulating as the average TV shoot-'em-up. All you need to start populating a white or lightly colored wall with imaginary figures is a good, bright light that can be easily moved. Position the lamp to cast the resulting shadows with maximum effectiveness while the performing 'artist' works in a comfortable position and begin. It's that simple.

"Once you've mastered the trick of creating several basic forms, the real fun of animating the characters begins by wiggling your thumbs and fingers. You'll soon be able to make your figures move, talk, eat and react in a surprisingly life-like manner. Complete the illusion with sound effects and you'll be the absolute center of attention."

The theory goes that if a child has a choice between a room full of glossy toys and a room full of cardboard boxes, he will invariably choose the latter. Perhaps one thing that is probably true about children is that they can amuse themselves with sticks and stones and lumps of clay. With bottles and jars and jugs and tubes.

Give a child a log and a plank, and he will invent a seesaw. Give him a box for a train. A rug for a desert.

Give him anything and he will transform it. Give him time on his hands and he will use it; he will re-create it.

Surely adults are different. We gear-up for our pleasure and recreation. Even our exercise. Few of us would admit that inducements for exercise and recreation drop before our fingertips. But not Lee Messing of Kew Gardens, New York, who finds recreation in "physical solitaire."

She reports that "over a period of twenty-eight years of married life, my husband and I have covered a million or more topics, settling and unsettling all kinds of problems.

"On this particular evening our talk led to 'self-improvement' and we agreed that most of the time it can be achieved with amounts of determination depending upon the situation. In my case, however, my husband felt that my physical involvement surely could not be extended or improved upon simply because there are only twenty-four hours in each day. Being an ardent tennis player, a long-distance swimmer with walking as part of my routine, and having a daily exercise program, his contention seemed quite logical. But as he was saying this, with my head still nodding in agreement, a small flame was kindled in my brain. I felt challenged. I tried to explain this to him, but he remained adamant in his belief, bringing all kinds of examples into the conversation relating specific instances when there simply hadn't been enough time.

"Well, I still felt that no matter how small the physical output, more could be introduced into the daily routine. We finally decided to make a bet.

"The following morning I immediately set forth to see what could be done. A dinner out on the town still excites me.

"Usually I start the day with my cup of Postum, my share of food supplements, while listening to the news on the radio. Rather than yawning or staring at my plants waiting for the water to come to a boil, I decided to do some leg kicks. Holding on to the back of the kitchen stool I pulled up my knee to meet my chin and then threw the leg all the way back. I managed to get in twenty of these on each foot easily. I had scored and I felt great!

"After my early morning tennis game, followed by chores around the house and my brief calisthenics routine, I left for a visit to my friend Ann, which is a two-mile walk from my house to a lovely residential section of my town. This usually allows for meditation and such. Today I decided that this stretch could be improved by jogging at least part of the distance. Instead of tiring me, to my delight, this only stimulated me, and my heart pounded pleasantly. I realized that I could increase the jogging gradually until one day perhaps I could make it all the way to Ann's. Hopefully she would understand my disarray upon arrival.

"During the next few hours my little game came to a standstill, since they were spent with people, and I did not feel ready to share my regimen as yet.

"Having finished my errands I found myself alone once again with some parcels, waiting for a bus to take me home. Here was another opportunity! No need to lean against a fence impatiently. I began pacing around in a circle keeping vigil for the arrival of the bus. Half of the walking I did on my toes, the other half I did almost on my heels—all this with my stomach muscles well

12-5: Lee Messing "moving."

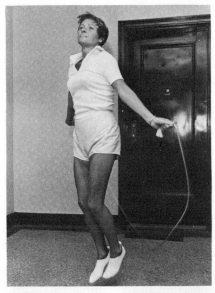

12-6: Lee Messing jumping.

12-7: Lee Messing playing.

tensed. This turned out to be a great way to pass the fifteen minutes in a much better way.

"Other improvisations followed that evening and by bedtime I was aware of the very best part of my new program even that first day and more so in the days to follow: my energy level had risen above its usual mark and I felt more alive than ever. To count the different ways of physical self-improvement is impossible; each one will find his own means. All I can say is that I found the effort well worth the result. Even sitting at my 'dinner on the town' I could still wiggle my toes under the table."

Surely recreation at its best is not setting up of schedules, is not intense activities engaged in a couple of times a week, is not a habit one must indulge in for the sake of health. Rather, recreation should be a full-bodied activity of pleasure, a challenge, a quest. A dimension we take our mind and body through. In the fundamental sense, recreation represents activities which allow us to re-create ourselves, to find pleasure in the simple things, to be like little children.

Take Mildred Graham of Chester, Connecticut, who reports that "Two years ago my husband retired and we planned our days including walks in our small village. We forgot that climbing hills could be so taxing—besides, I talked to everyone that we met. Therefore, we didn't feel that physical exercise was present. So we set up a walking plan in our cellar. We have a fifty-foot house and forty-four times around a course of obstacles like a ping-pong table, heater, work bench, etc., equals one mile. We do this mile two or three times per day with great speed—swinging our arms and to music. However, sometimes we play what we call town games or syllable games, shouting them at each other as we pass in opposite directions. The towns—we take a letter of the alphabet and name towns or cities from all forty-eight states, which we have been in at some time or other. But the syllables are fun, too, like yesterday we had 'mar,' we use words with 'mar' or a saying with 'mar.' Example: Marwall, market, etc."

It seems that when we "let down" our defenses, when we act spontaneously, we frequently engage in activities that are playful in a fundamental, primitive sense. When we let our hair down, our bodies take over.

Nancy Hetherington reports that "Some time before lunch each day I put on some very 'up and lively' music and begin running around, hopping, skipping, kicking, jumping, or whatever creative way my body wants to move. I keep moving for twenty minutes (my goal is thirty). My children love it. Either they participate or sit back, clap, and let me entertain them."

In the state of Washington, in the shadow of Mt. Rainier, Mrs. Mary R. Leason retires to a secluded spot and does her bird walk. "I lift up my arms," she reports, "like the birds lift up their wings. I inhale and exhale more deeply. Then after I take all the oxygen I need for my lungs, I walk slowly, looking at dandelions. I need nothing else."

chapter 13

The Body

by Malcolm Wells

"Every man
is the builder
of a temple,
called his body,
to the god he worships,
after a style purely his own,
nor can he get off
by hammering marble instead.
We are all sculptors
and painters,
and our material
is our own flesh and blood
and bones."

Henry Thoreau
Walden

Having read this far, you are fired with enthusiasm, determined to get more involved in recreation and play, and eager to see that the spaces needed for healthful, lifetime sports are provided in your neighborhood. You're thinking, in fact, of attending next week's city council meeting, when suddenly a peal of laughter yanks you back into the present moment.

You'd forgotten you were traveling, hadn't you? Forgotten you and 112 other people were flying together. Here you are, seven miles above the green American land, and here *he* is, seven inches away, laughing his fool head off. The young man seated immediately to your right is wearing a pair of the complimentary earphones the stewardess distributed before takeoff, and he chuckles and then laughs heartily in response to something coming to him through the plastic tubes. So absorbed is he, in fact, by the airline humor, that you are free to inspect him in some detail . . .

About thirty years old. A smoker. A bit overweight. Not an athlete, not by a long shot. He looks like a happy, uncomplicated person.

Unable to restrain your curiosity, you reach for the in-flight magazine to see if it carries a clue to the source of all this laughter. Page 76 is entitled "Audio Entertainment." You check the selections . . .

Symphonic Patterns. No.
Latin Sound. No.
Hawaiian Melodies. Not that one, either.
Comedy.—Laughtime interspersed with music. Aha!

As you begin to congratulate yourself on the quality of your detective work you notice that the laughter beside you suddenly ends. The comedy, it seems, has just undergone its first musical interspersal. The young man flips impatiently through the pages of a magazine as music you cannot hear fills his head. Now, apparently, the music ends. The magazine is tossed aside and soon the laughter returns.

The Need to Play

Is this *play* you're witnessing? It certainly isn't work. No effort of any kind is required. But if it is play, what a passive kind of play it is! There's no imagination, no creativity, no exploration, no challenge involved. All it takes is the ability to sit in one spot with earphones in your ears and let a lot of carefully-programmed and laugh-tracked funny stuff be pumped into your head. It seems a waste, our being reduced to this level of activity, and yet how creative can one be while locked for three hours inside a roaring tube full of highly inflammable fuel with 112 strangers? It's the modern dilemma in a nutshell, the price of our success. Our spoonfed society, which has produced the wonder of the modern airplane, has also produced the paunchy young man on your right, and the electronic humor that so titillates him.

We want—and need—very much to play, but as we move closer to becoming a leisure-time people we find play itself harder and harder to arrange. Instead, we play more and more vicariously, by watching others play on television, by having our own thoughts and actions replaced by packaged thoughts and other people's actions. Perhaps that's the unavoidable price of living in a high-energy society. Perhaps. But a lot of people believe we're on the verge of a great turnaround, a great rejection of this whole phony, sick, plastic mess.

By today's standards, play isn't even respectable, not for adults at any rate. Our puritanical notions die hard. Margaret Mead notes that "financial support for the study of play among adults has generally been available to social scientists only when play has been called recreation, a label that identifies its role in recreating human beings for the serious and proper business of life."

It's sad. And even sadder, perhaps, is the fact that in today's world, play *is* needed for that very purpose, for re-creating us to endure life's boring and serious work. So we have a doubled need for play—to make life endurable now, and to lead us into a playful, happy future. "No happy man ever disturbed a meeting," said A. S. Neill, "or preached a war, or lynched a Negro."

But we're too embarrassed to play. If we're not wearing $75 worth of appropriate sports attire, we won't consider making fools of ourselves by running on the earth or throwing things to each other. And the thought of *touching* each other! Heavens! We get old too soon. Psycho-sclerosis, Ashley Montague calls it, hardening of the spirit. Only after we've had a few drinks do we dare to drop our tight little masks and play a bit. And only then will society tolerate our foolishness.

Most of the studies you read on the phenomenon of play are written by social psychologists. (Our lack of playfulness probably has a lot to do with the fact that social psychologists have appeared on the scene.) They all agree that play is a vital activity, that it is an important part of what we are, of how we function as a race, but what unplayful reports the social psychologists write! Everything is couched in the most humorless of terms, as if to assure the reader that no fun was allowed to creep into the project. And the language! Edwin Newman would cringe to read

13-1: The Hands.

13-2: The Legs.

such deadly jargon, with all its talk of conflict utilization, learning sessions, and facilitatorship. Oh, yes, and let us not overlook commonality of spirit and interpersonal relationships. Social researchers and educators who write about play seem never to have learned the basic lesson taught by the subject. They seem bent on crushing all spontaneity, all inventiveness, all fun, out of it.

"Play," to most of them, is used in the sense of game-playing, of following someone else's rules, of submitting to organized, even compulsory, recreation. But is that what play is all about? Not to most people. They never mention organized play. "A frisbee, soft grass, bare feet, two people." That's what comes to mind when Sam is asked about play. To Karen it's hide and seek, or playing tag. Susan thinks of dancing—alone—to her favorite music. And old Harry likes to run along the edge of the sea, feeling the great, naked earth moving by beneath his feet. Then he falls to the sand, panting, and enjoys monitoring all the thumping and the huffing he hears, as the dependable old systems restore energy to his muscles. That's when his high sets in. That's when he can most enjoy the miracles all around him. He is, for a little while, one with them.

The freest kind of play is the play in which no responsibilities are involved. No responsibility, that's the key. No hassles. But if we are to play our lives away, who, then, will be responsible? Answer: everyone. When life is fun and interesting, when everyone happily lends a hand, the pressure of responsibility ends.

You should meet the people who run a little country concrete company in Ohio. They have fun all the time, by which I don't mean to imply that they never stop laughing, that they go around with idiotic grins plastered across their cheeks. After all, having fun can be very serious business. It's the light in their eyes that tells the story. The night the huge new cement tower rolled off the trailer in the snowstorm and clanked its way downhill in the darkness toward a farmhouse became a night of play for those Ohioans. They had a ball. Soaked, frozen, tired, they worked till dawn, enjoying every minute, seeing the ridiculous side of it all, and the satisfying side of doing it well. They didn't know that all the rest of us groan and suffer in the face of dilemmas half as large. Or maybe they did know, and knowing, decided on a better way.

13-3: The Peace.

13-4: The Leap.

Playing with Life

Rather than the usual alternatives of work, as opposed to play, *problems* vs. *fun* might be more accurate. When the consequences of an activity get too heavy, too troublesome, too complicated—when it becomes monotonous—all the fun goes away and it becomes tiring and unpleasant. It becomes, in fact, what most of us call work. The amount of energy expended has, apparently, nothing to do with it. It's all in how you look at it.

Someone said that it wasn't until he heard a private letter of his read in a public courtroom that the difference between work and play really dawned on him: play stops when fun disappears, and his fun had just flown out the window. It needn't have, of course; if he'd looked more objectively at the situation he might have had a ball. There are gold mines of fun in pompous places. But we can't blame him for squirming a bit as a lawyer pumped all the sarcasm he could muster into the reading of that letter. The writer of the letter could see, as he looked around the courtroom, that to most members of this straight-laced society of ours, the idea of anyone putting lighthearted comments (like the ones just then being read aloud) into a business letter was a real no-no. Work is supposed to be serious, sober, dull . . . right? Just listen to us: "Thank God it's Friday."

Until he'd experienced his few minutes of embarrassment there in the courtroom, the writer of funny business letters had never worked a day in his life. As an architect, he'd put in long hours every day of his career, but every minute had been fun, interesting. Long hours hadn't made it hard. They'd only made it more rewarding. Only a dose of oppressive humorlessness could take the edge away.

"But then," you may be thinking, "he, as an architect, didn't have to sit in a factory every day of his life, putting widgets on gadgets." True, but there are also a lot of happy, smiling, playful widget-installers. They know the secret. They turn boredom into play by letting their own personal copies of this marvelously inventive thing called the human mind fantasize about some of the millions of variations possible within the limited world of widget-watching.

The very purpose of life almost seems to be to have fun, to play, to retain our youthfulness, even at fifty—or eighty. Read

Warren Stetzel's *School for The Young** if you want to see just
how important—how vital—it is that we retain the quality of
youth throughout a lifetime. Most of us have that youthfulness
squeezed out during a decade and a half of schooling. It dries up
before the television set. And we bore each other, old by the age
of thirty.

The alternative to our dreary fate seems to lie in play, not
in mainlining soda pop and hallucinogens while lying on satin
pillows, watching television, but in finding the interesting, the
funny, or even the exciting aspects of whatever activity is at
hand.

Let us suppose, for instance, that you have just finished
reading this delightful book. Suppose, too, that you have no other
books with you, and that you must now spend two hours in a
dreary waiting room until a friend arrives to pick you up. What
happens? If you're tired, and if sleep is possible, you may let
yourself slip into unconsciousness there. But sleep at such times
is often impossible, and it is, after all, a waste of time if you are
not tired, especially when there are so many exciting things to do.
If you don't know about them, of course you will be bored, or
frustrated, and little streams of excess acid will pour into your
stomach.

Some of the easy and obvious ways to play while waiting are
simply to watch the other people, to listen to what they are saying.
You can guess their ages, try to identify their careers and their
accents, their relationships to one another . . . any number of
things about them. Or you can study the room in which you are
temporarily confined. Chances are it's one of the ugliest rooms in
America. (Waiting rooms are usually the worst rooms of all.)
Try to figure out why it is ugly. What is it that actually makes one
room depressing and another, similar, room appealing? You can
play detective, and study the scratches on the furniture around
you, to see who and what used it before you. You can listen for all
the background noises, and try to identify them—close your eyes
and think about what the blind see through their other senses.
And then, of course, you can turn to an examination of that most
fascinating of all subjects, yourself. There's enough material there
for a month of study, or a year, let alone a mere two hours.

---

* Celo Press, Burnsville, N.C. 28714, Pprbk., 224 pp., $4.00.

13-5: The Flight.

But is all this really play, or merely chewing gum? Is it simply a way to avoid boredom? Perhaps. But "simply" avoiding boredom isn't as simple as it sounds. When the mind is active, exploring—learning without pressure—not only boredom but time, too, disappears, and the discoveries made there amidst the asphalt tile and the cigarette butts lead outward and outward toward new worlds, new activities. It seems that we were given the capacity for play for just that purpose—to expand ourselves forever toward the possible.

If you must address five hundred envelopes in an afternoon, or run in place for twenty minutes, or wait at the end of a long line, the likelihood of catching a dose of boredom is high, but if you remember to explore all the facets of a situation, if you fantasize—if you *play*—then you're likely to enjoy it, and learn something new at the same time.

No, it's not just chewing gum, or baby-sitting your mind; it's like money in the bank, only better. If you can make yourself a happier, brighter person—and if you can help others, too—think what a promise that holds out for our future! If we are to avoid becoming a race of nuclear-powered, laugh-cued zombies, we will not manage it by waiting for word from above—from government, from advertising, from television. We will do it by setting free these marvelous animals that we are, and letting them expand in all their best directions.

Fun, or play, or recreation, of course, is a very serious business. Watch a child at play if you need proof. It isn't play to her, you see; it's real life. It's how she learns about our world. Kids like best to play where they can see us doing the things they think they're doing, too. The sidewalks of New York are in some ways far richer playgrounds than the fields of Nebraska, and at least one gifted educator, noting the speed with which kids learn by example, feels that in most cases they'd get better educations by growing directly into the adult world, without school. The growth and the play need never stop.

"I never worked harder," said a friend, "than I did during that week at the beach when I built all those giant pyramids. For ten hours each day, almost without stopping, I moved between six and eight tons of sand, using nothing but a little flat stick to do it, and I loved every minute. I'd started that vacation worn out, but each day, there I was, up at dawn ready for a new

13-6: The Bird.

13-7: The Climb.

round of discovery and exploration. I couldn't believe that I'd managed to live fifty-one years without ever once before discovering the pure, uncomplicated joy of building simple classical forms in damp sand—or the joy of watching the tide slowly turn them back into the perfection of uncluttered beach again. I came away with a much deeper respect for the wonders of antiquity, for sand, for light and shade, and, I must say, even for myself.

"I won't bore you with all the lessons I learned while playing there, but I can assure you that during that wonderful week the things I learned opened up new worlds for me. Now I'm deep into a study of early civilizations, a subject for which I had no interest at all before. And I can't wait till next summer. Part of the fun, I suppose, was in the way the architectural forms tended to attract other beautiful forms, but the pyramids alone would have been enough."

No two people seem to agree as to the exact nature of this great life-need called play, but all agree that it is indeed a universal, human physical need. What is this bag of flesh that cries and sings and responds to music? What is this thing that *plays?* Layers beyond layers exist in us, but who can say which of them, if any, is in ultimate control? All we know is that the play-need is there among them somewhere. This fine machine, beyond all computers, all rocket ships, is, as Thoreau said, our temple. We are what we eat, that's true, but we are what we play as well.

The human body is a source of endless fascination to us all, a fact easily proved by a glance at any magazine rack. Except perhaps for food, the body is the number-one subject of interest to the race. Most other things get valued in relation to it. The body, when it's in good condition, and in motion, enchants us. Some of our rapture, of course, is pure lust, a spectator-type phenomenon of great value. But lust by no means accounts for all of this powerful interest we share. There seems to be a huge and untapped area of *a*sexual body-interest in addition to the all-too-present sexual kind. How it is to be tapped remains to be seen, but it appears that in play we come closest to finding the way. Watching the body at play—graceful, unmannered, free, without malice—is almost as pleasant as being at play.

Artists see the beautiful in every human form, and, when they're successful, they make us see it, too. They see beyond the cover-girl glossiness we're programmed to applaud, and show us the miracles at hand.

13-8: The Track.

Can you still remember the thrill of your first solo bike ride? Of learning to drive? Each new skill was really a combination of thousands, of legions of nerve cells and muscles learning to accomplish, automatically, feats of balance, measurement, timing, and judgement beyond our understanding. The excitement of each new success gave us hints, at least, of all the wonders behind it, before it was tucked away into automation and forgotten. In play those thrills continue, as we explore further into what for each of us is the unknown. "Man's capacities have never been measured," said Thoreau, "nor are we to judge of what he can do, so little has been tried." The inventor plays in his workshop, the gymnast plays on the bars, the child plays at the curb. Each is exploring his personal unknown, growing toward those unmeasured capacities.

The uninitiated are shocked and repelled—and frightened—as they witness a surgical operation. What at first look like purpled masses of chicken parts slowly change, as familiarity grows, into beautiful creations. The operation is almost over before the observer perceives that he has witnessed a bloody miracle, and he never again looks in the mirror without remembering the things unseen behind the skin.

The Body

For all our surface acquaintance with the more public regions of the human skin, its naked presence still shocks us. For anyone out of touch with locker rooms, a first visit is a stunning reminder of what it is we keep hidden by our clothes, for here is the human animal as it looks in America during the latter part of the twentieth century. Overfed, underused, it is that ancient animal nonetheless, the mammal that stood erect and fought its way to world supremacy for a time. Seen in that light, all the paunches, hair, muscles, and organs become fascinating. It's like having a front-row seat in the hall of evolution.

Maybe it's time we went back to the original meaning of the word "gymnasium" (to train, naked). When we're not having the most fun of all, playing life, then the next best fun is learning bodies—our own and each other's. Tension, grace, beauty, movement, poetry, speed, coordination, comedy, exhaustion . . . the whole range of human activity is manifest—or implied—in play, in free play of any kind, uninhibited. That's what this book is all about, not just getting your exercise, but trying to be more fully, again, the free, happy animal with the vast potential. Is it possible? Of course not. Like every other goal it is a target, unattainable, but any movement in its direction is bound to be an improvement—in health, in happiness, and in the direction and fate of the race.

Little kids play at life, pretending to be what *we* are. We marvel at their energy. We can't pretend to be what we are, so we go exploring, with a ball, with a bike, with a shovel, with a paint brush, or with only our imagination, pushing out the boundaries of whatever we do. We can't all go exploring in the wilderness anymore, there's too little of it left, so we go exploring all the uncharted areas close at hand, passively, when action is impossible, or actively, as in free, full-body play.

Someday, perhaps during our lifetimes, if the life-movement continues its lusty growth, the towns and cities of America will be all vine-draped and meadowed, ready for healthful outdoor play. The underground architecture movement alone is likely to return thousands and thousands of asphalted acres to life. All we need is a clear choice, a choice between dead, polluted, ugly cities, and clean, healthful, beautiful cities, and we'll make the right decision. We'll no longer have to set aside old railroad beds or unused corners of shopping centers for play. Acres of gardens and lawns, forests and wildflowers, will lie at our doorsteps. Imagine running to work—in bare feet! And then discovering that work wasn't work any more! But that's all decades away, and we are living now. We've got to get started, any way we can, and launch the playful, free, nonaggressive society of the future. Launching it won't all be a bed of roses, you know. What if, after years of effort, after starting with the old railroad rights-of-way and then graduating to the great garden-covered cities, we were still hung up on our rigid, don't-touch-me attitudes? What then? Wouldn't it all have been for nothing?

Stiffness, exclusivity, hostility, violence—they're the price of growth without play. Win-at-any-cost, instead of win-a-few, lose-a-few. But our shells will not crack easily, having grown for so long. For all our talk of freedom we still manage to enjoy each other's minds and bodies only at a distance, at football games, or in the movies, or on television. We see this tightness in ourselves

13-9: The Sea.

13-10: The Rope.

and hate it, but don't know what to do. Each of us waits for someone else to take the first step. After you, Alphonse.

Take hugging, for example. It's slowly making a comeback, slowly knocking down a few of our unwanted barriers, winning converts as it goes. Some of the world's stiffest hugs can be seen taking place in America today, but each one is a little less stiff than the one before. It's fun to watch a real macho type get trapped into his first public embrace. Any show of fear is taboo under his code, so, challenged, he's forced to do what he thinks only women and sissies do. His first man-hug is the hug of a cardboard robot, and he looks stricken, Archie Bunker out of his depth. But afterward he talks about it—a lot. He makes jokes about the weird custom, but he comes back next time, and the next, until at last his facade melts away and he discovers that it is no loss at all, that he has not become something he didn't want to be.

Organic Play

Hugging . . . jogging . . . more comfortable, less formal clothes . . . bike-traffic jams . . . books like this one . . . all around us we see evidence of freedom—of naturalness—trying to reassert itself. It is the opposite of war, so it must be a kind of peace. Maybe the sixties got us turned around. It's hard to say, but it seems certain that whatever did it, it's all part of the life-movement we see expressed in what at first seem to be unrelated ways . . . organic gardening, solar energy, health foods, conservation, windpower, and "lawns" of wildflowers.

- We jog in the park only to find that the streams are dead, so our new jogging-powered energies get directed toward sewerless toilets, or politics, or better detergents, or the reduction of fertilizer runoff from lawns and farms—or toward any of the interrelated phenomena that affect streams in such vital ways.

- We ride our new bikes into town and are appalled by all the erosion caused by overpaving. We become paving-control enthusiasts while we play.

- We find that our kids are bored to death by the dreary stuff being forced upon them in their dreary elec-

13-11: The Roll.

tronic classrooms, where play has no place in the education process, and we bend the stiff board-of-education members a little at the next meeting.

- We decide to skip the all-day sports telecast this Saturday and insulate the attic instead, only to discover that that grimy, itchy job is more fun than tube-watching would have been. The Big Saturday Game, this week, has us pitted against Heat Loss itself, and the contest seems undecided until, at the last minute before dinner, we sweep around their extreme right end, plug that last gap, and win the prize of low fuel bills for the first straight year in a row.

On television we see The Good Life made of sugar-loaded soft drinks, headache medicine, big cars, and sleeping pills. Out the window, we see The Good Life made of sunlight and rain, of green plants and an endlessly-changing pageant that thrives somehow, still, in spite of us. And here, indoors, we see mixed blessings: the trappings of material wealth along with an expanding waistline and shortness of breath. Life, somehow, isn't all it was cracked up to be. Now they say there may be cancer-causing agents in the drinking water. How can we think about play, with things like that hanging over us? It's hard enough just to live, without also having to find extra time for play. Tonight's news was awful, and you want us to play? To ride a bike and have fun and hug people? What are you, crazy?

It's a mixed bag, life, isn't it? And each of us tends to see only the side at hand, like one of the twelve blind men who stood in a circle around an elephant, touching it, and describing an animal far different from the one described by each of the others. Seldom do we see the whole picture unified, one. But it *is* all one, and if we are about to launch an organic era, we'd better train ourselves to see it. We can't have it both ways. We can't have good health and sugar-coated cereals, bright skies and Detroit engines.

We really are at the threshold of what could be an organic era. It's not certain, yet, which must come first, the green cities or the healthy attitudes, but it seems to be the latter. If we can break away, somehow, and get started in the right direction, we can play our way into paradise.

Appendix

Chapter Three: The Trail

TRAIL ORGANIZATIONS

Appalachian Trail Conference
P. O. Box 236
Harpers Ferry, W.Va. 25425

Potomac Appalachian Trail Club
1718 N Street, NW
Washington, D.C. 20036

Appalachian Mountain Club
5 Joy Street
Boston, Mass. 02108

Green Mountain Club
108 Merchants Row
Rutland, Vt. 05701

Keystone Trails Association
RD 1, Box 91—Ramick Road
Temple, Pa. 19560

New York-New Jersey Trail
    Conference
GPO Box 2250
New York, N.Y. 10001

Old Dominion Trail Club
Box 25283
Richmond, Va. 23260

Mountain Club of Maryland
6608 Carroll Hts. Road
Skyesville, Md. 21784

West Virginia Scenic Trails
    Association
P. O. Box 4042
Charleston, W.Va. 25304

Wilmington Trail Club
Box 1184
Wilmington, Del. 19899

Florida Trail Association
4410 NW 18th Place
Gainesville, Fla. 32605

Georgia Appalachian Trail Club
1351 Springdale Rd., NE
Atlanta, Ga. 30306

Tennessee Eastman Hiking Club
Tennessee Eastman Company
Kingsport, Tenn. 37662

The Prairie Club
38 So. Dearborn St.
Room 1010
Chicago, Ill. 60603

Historical Hiking Trails, Inc.
P. O. Box 17507
Memphis, Tenn. 38117

Kentucky Trails Coordinator
Department of Parks—11th Floor
Capital Plaza Tower
Frankfort, Ky. 40601

Louisiana Trails Advisory Council
P. O. Box 44361
Baton Rouge, La. 70804

Missouri Trails Association
Box 9958
Kansas City, Mo. 64134

The Ozark Society
Box 2914
Little Rock, Ark. 72203

Michigan Heritage Trails
973 East Maple Street
Holly, Mich. 48442

Buckeye Trail Association
P. O. Box 254
Worthington, Ohio 43085

Texas Forestry Association
Box 1488
Lufkin, Texas 75901

Kansas Capitols Trails
Box 1
Tecumseh, Kansas 66542

Montana Wilderness Association
P. O. Box 548
Bozeman, Mont. 59715

Colorado Mountain Trails
  Foundation
Box 2238
Littleton, Colorado 80161

Wasatch Mountain Club
425 So. 8th W.
Salt Lake City, Utah 84106

Mormon Pioneer Trail
135 So. State Street
Salt Lake City, Utah 84111

Trail Club of Oregon
P. O. Box 1243
Portland, Ore. 97207

Washington Alpine Club
P. O. Box 352
Seattle, Wash. 98111

Southern Arizona Hiking Club
P. O. Box 12122
Tucson, Ariz. 85711

Pacific Crest Trail System
  Conference
Hotel Green
Pasadena, Calif. 91104

Berkeley Hiking Club
P. O. Box 147
Berkeley, Calif. 94701

Chapter Five: The Course

Parcours Ltd.
3701 Buchanan St.
San Francisco, Calif. 94123

Recreation Development Corporation (Fit-Trail)
932 Ideal Way
Charlotte, N.C. 28203

Landscape Structure, Inc.
300 Dawn Heather Drive
Delano, Minn. 55328

Distributor: Ross/Recreation Equipment
P. O. Box 642
Tiburon, Calif. 94920

LifeCourse Resource Center
Management Sciences for Health
One Broadway
Cambridge, Md. 02142

Chapter Eight: The Dance

SOME QUESTIONS AND ANSWERS: FOLK DANCE

How can I find out about folk dance groups in my area?
Consult one of the following publications:

Folk Dance Directory
P.O. Box 500
Midwood Station
Brooklyn, New York 11230
Phone: 212-434-1766

An annual guide to classes,
activities, periodicals, services,
products, and contact people.
Covers the entire United
States and parts of Canada.
$.60 a copy

Mixed Pickles   A monthly newspaper for spe-
Same address as above   cial events. Covers eastern
                                     and   western   United   States,
                                     and foreign events.

$4.00 a year

A membership in Folk Dance Association includes both
of the above-mentioned periodicals, plus discounts on folk
dance tours, camps, weekends, and other activities.
Same address as above   *$6.00 a year*

Midwest:
Viltis—a folklore magazine. Contains worldwide news
about ethnic happenings, travel with the accent on folk
dance. Also, foreign cuisine, recipes, researched articles
about dances, and folklore of all nations.

V. F. Beliajus, Editor
P.O. Box 1226
Denver, Colorado 80201
Phone: 303-534-2025

Northwest:
Northwest Folkdancer
Box 30663
Seattle, Washington 98103
Phone: 206-827-5587

West Coast:
Folk Dance Federation of California
1095 Market St.
San Francisco, California
Phone: 415-431-8717

Worldwide Dancing:
B. Stewart
P.O. Box 8033
Columbus, Ohio 43201
Phone: 614-299-1085

How can I start a folk dance group in my community?

Assuming that you know some folk dances, start a class with a few friends. You can popularize your class by the following methods:

1. Word of mouth
2. Post notices in churches, synagogues, supermarkets, bulletin boards in projects, and community centers.
3. Advertise in folk periodicals, in local newspapers, on local radio stations that announce events as a community service.
4. Get mailing lists from folk festival councils in your area.

Once you have a class, form a demonstration group and perform for community organizations, PTA, teenage clubs, senior citizen clubs, etc. After the performance, have the dancers invite the audience to join in a few simple dances. Finally, distribute handbills, giving time and place for classes.

Hold ethnic festivals and invite the various ethnic groups in your area to participate with musicians, singers, and dancers in costume. Decorate for the occasion with Japanese lanterns, Polish paper cut-outs, Ukranian Easter eggs, etc. Have booths selling foods, ethnic jewelry, handicrafts, etc. Involve teenage groups, clubs, schools.

How can I find an appropriate space for my folk dance group?
Contact:
Department of real estate
Parks department
City planning commission
Sanitation department

The following places are usually free; a permit is needed.
Parks
Playgrounds on weekends
Closed off streets
Shopping malls and plazas (parking areas on Sundays)
Vacant lots
Waterfront areas (a non-profit organization renovating the
South Street Seaport in New York City, to be used as a

cultural center, permitted dance teachers to hold folk dance sessions along the waterfront during the summer months.)

Spaces to rent:
  Community centers
  Synagogues and churches
  YM & YWCA
  Ballrooms

The following should also be investigated:
  Housing projects
  High school adult centers
  Senior citizen centers

What equipment is needed?
  A califone
  A public address system
  Folk dance records which can be purchased from:
    Worldtone Folk Music Int'l
    Kenneth Spear
    230 Seventh Ave.
    New York, New York 10011

    Rhythms Productions
    Box 34485
    Whitney Building
    Los Angeles, California 90034